Fibromyalg

You Have the Power to Heal Yourself

A Remarkable Fibromyalgia Recovery Story
Showing That Fibromyalgia is
Not an Incurable Illness.

by

Victoria B. Allen

Co-Author Christine Clayfield

The reader should also be aware that while web addresses or any prices mentioned were correct at the time of writing, they may become out of date in the future.

Author: Victoria B. Allen
Co-Author: Christine Clayfield

Table of Contents

Table of Contents 3

Foreword And Why I Wrote This Book...6

Co-Author Christine Clayfield 8

Chapter 1: The Fascinating Fascia World...9

1.Fibromyalgia... 9

2. Fascia... 10

3. Myofascial Pain 21

4. Myofascial Release 26

5. The Importance of Stretching 36

Chapter 2: Mind-Body Connection..44

Chapter 3: The First Ouch & The Shifting Sands 47

Chapter 4: Hidden Dangers...51

1. The Medical Opinion... 51

2. The Environment 52

3. Toxic Overload.. 60

4. The Self-Fulfilling Prophecy.. 62

Chapter 5: You ARE Powerful! 64

1. You Are the Master... 64

2. Super Syndrome... 65

3. The Power of Acceptance 67

4. The Power of Positive Thinking.. 68

Chapter 6: Motivational Swear Words...75

Chapter 7: The Life Race and Your Mind 78

Chapter 8: Fibro Recovery on a Small Budget 81

1. Attitude Adjustment... 81

2. Immerse Yourself in Nature 86

3. The Power of Music *89*

4. The Power of Laughter *95*

5. Home Life Adjustment *96*

6. Take a Breath *108*

7. Food Choices *109*

8. The Power of Intermittent Fasting *115*

9. Myofascial Release at Low Cost *116*

Chapter 9: Pills, Potions and Paraphernalia 121

1. Pills *121*

2. FDA Approved for Fibromyalgia *122*

3. What About Vitamin Pills? *124*

4. Potions *125*

5. Paraphernalia *129*

Chapter 10: Find *Your* Mantra 136

Chapter 11: Find the Funny Side of Life 138

Chapter 12: What Makes You Happy? 141

Chapter 13: Therapy Treatments 144

1. Yoga Therapy *144*

2. Qigong and Tai Chi *145*

3. Massage Therapy *145*

4. Counselling Therapy *146*

5. Sensory Deprivation Therapy - Floating *148*

6. Hydrotherapy *150*

7. Infrared Sauna Therapy *151*

8. Aromatherapy *153*

9. Scalar Wave Therapy *155*

10. Other Therapies to Consider *158*

Chapter 14: Step Out of Character 162

Chapter 15: Just Say NO! 165

Chapter 16: Weird & Wonderful Wellness 167

Chapter 17: YOLO – Embrace It! 169

Chapter 18: Are You Surprized? 170

1. How Do You Get Fibromyalgia? 170

2. Where Do You Start? 172

Chapter 19: What to Expect on Your Recovery Journey? 173

1. What Mindset Do You Need Do Be Successful? 173

2. Don't ever give up 176

5. What is Likely to Work Best For Me? 177

6. How Long Will it Take To Be Pain Free? 177

7. Knowledge is Power 178

8. You Are the Lucky One! 178

9. A State of Mind 178

Chapter 20: Remember! 180

Resources & References 182

Foreword And Why I Wrote This Book

I am Victoria B. Allen and I live in Canada. I **was** a fibromyalgia sufferer who has walked the path of this bizarre and often brutal malady for many years. I am motivated to share insights through my personal story in the hope that what I have learned during this black time in my life will help others navigate the fibromyalgia maze with a lighter heart, more ease and an accelerated recovery time.

I presume that you had all medical tests carried out, that your health care provider could not provide a medical explanation for your symptoms and that you have been informed that there is no cause for fibromyalgia and no cure. I am here to tell you a different story because I suffered with fibromyalgia for a few years and now I am very happy to tell you that I have no more pain at all!

This book is about chronic, unexplained pain and my personal journey about what I did to treat myself. Within the following pages I outline both free and purchased products and treatments I used when searching for relief, and how I also found many treatment options that really helped at zero cost.

When it comes down to healing my body, I'm all about *"outside of the box"* because my experience has taught me that those who challenge the status quo and regularly think a little differently from the masses (those who may continue to rely upon traditional and often outdated medical opinions or practices) often have a far more expedient recovery rate, no matter what might ail you. All you need is an open mind, a real desire to recover as quickly as possible and a belief that it IS possible to be pain free. My personal story with fibromyalgia will help to lift you out of the depths of despair you may be feeling. You will begin to move forward with a plan of renewed optimism once you see for yourself that **yes you can** get your life back.

This book will help anyone diagnosed with fibromyalgia to feel motivated, positive, powerful and less stressed because despite what the mainstream medical community may say about this chronic condition, **you have the power to heal yourself.**

Recovering will take time and to achieve success, you will have to be committed to putting some time and effort into it. However, the rewards are many and you will be proud of yourself, and all you have accomplished.

Perhaps you've been diagnosed with fibro and your health care provider has told you that there is little to be done, except manage this malady the best way you can. Rather than simply accepting that this life of pain will be what you can wake up to for the rest of your life, why not take a more proactive approach instead? This book is about how I did just that, and more.

Why not take control of your own health story because once you realize how powerful you really are, you can choose to change your story and live the life you truly want. Instead of enduring a life of pain that constantly gets you out of bed on the wrong side and feeling anxious about every new day, why not choose to greet your mornings with a much more positive outlook that will help you to get your health back on track? Once you free yourself from daily fibro pain and feeling exhausted, your energy will return, and you will have much more time to really enjoy living your life. You will soon realize that all your efforts have been worth every minute of time spent.

Important note: I am not in any way a medically qualified individual and this book is not intended to give medical advice. The information contained within the pages of this book is a personal outline of my experience and knowledge and has been compiled to provide an overview of the subject and detail some personal experience of the symptoms, treatments and alternative therapies that are available. For a firm diagnosis of any health condition, and for a treatment plan suitable for you, before relying upon on any exercises or treatments outlined in this book, you should first consult your health care provider. Fascia or fascia problems by the way, do not show on MRI or XRAY machine.

I have deliberately repeated a few things in this book to stress the importance. The more you read the same thing, the better you will remember them. I am not going into detail about the history or research in this book. Nor will I expand a lot about the medical background surrounding fibro. There are plenty of books about that and a mass of information online. There are hardly any recovery stories therefore that's what I will focus on: your recovery.

There will be spaces throughout this book for you to write your own notes. Expect to have fun, connect with your creative self and enjoy moments where you simply forget about fibro, until the moments begin to be hours, then days, then weeks, then months, because (like myself) you have completely healed yourself.

Co-Author Christine Clayfield

Author Christine Clayfield has written Chapters 1, 2, 18, 19 and 20 of this book. Her knowledge far exceeds mine.

She **was** a fibromyalgia sufferer and has been studying fibromyalgia for 5 years. I was one of her first clients she took under her wing. She convinced me that I **can** be pain free and I believed her. She told me what to do for complete recovery, which I applied, and I am now pain free. Thank you again Christine!

Christine's fibromyalgia recovery knowledge is vast, and she is in the process of writing a book about it, which will include her own recovery journey. She is now a health coach and qualified to teach people about fascia and fibromyalgia as she has obtained, or is studying to obtain, several diplomas and certificates in the field. To name but a few:

- Certified Fibromyalgia Advisor Training Program Certificate
- Effective Pain Management Training Diploma
- Fascial Fitness Mentoring Diploma
- Fibromyalgia and Chronic Myofascial Pain Syndrome Course
- Fibromyalgia Syndrome Course Certificate
- Stress Management Course Diploma
- The Fibromyalgia Academy Recovery Program
- Time to Demystify Fibromyalgia Certificate

If you are interested in finding out when her book will be published, you can email her at info@christineclayfield.com. Christine is planning to do individual Zoom sessions to help people with fibromyalgia to achieve complete recovery. Email her if you are interested.

You can read Christine's life story in her book: "*No Fourth River*". This book was written **before** she was diagnosed fibromyalgia.

Keep reading to find out how I beat those ferocious fibro blues that according to the mainstream medical community were *"incurable"* and how, if I can completely treat myself and have no more pain, **YOU have the power to do the same for yourself.**

I hope your recovery journey to a pain free life will be as successful as my journey has been.

Victoria B. Allen

Chapter 1: The Fascinating Fascia World

by Christine Clayfield

It is important, before you read how fibromyalgia can be treated, that you know some important fibromyalgia related things. That's what this chapter is all about.

1.Fibromyalgia

The word *"Fibromyalgia"* needs to be broken down into 3 distinctly separate words because this will help to give you a clearer understanding of what this word really means without all the technical mumbo jumbo.

"Fibro" is a Latin word meaning *"fibrous tissues"* and fibrous tissues, when referring to a human body, simply means a strong, stretchy tissue that supports the bones and organs of the body.

"Myo" means muscle in Greek.

"Algia" is a Greek word meaning *"pain of unknown origin"*. These letters will be found attached to many different maladies such as *"arthralgia"* (joint pain), *"myalgia"* (muscle pain), cephalgia (headache pain), *"fibromyalgia"* (muscle, joint and tendon pain).

Therefore, fibromyalgia is very simplistically said: a medically unexplained pain that is caused by a stretchy tissue connected to a muscle.

You must be thinking, wow, lucky me (!) to have an unknown, chronic pain condition that affects muscles, joints and tendons all at the same time. Yes, I have thought this very same thing many times and have since retrained my mind to think differently because **when you change your thoughts, you change your world.**

The reality is that no good can come from simply believing and then accepting what many will say is an incurable, miserable and malicious malady that besides elevating pain to a never before experienced level in your life, is also often accompanied by a whole myriad of other debilitating conditions.

Who would also like to have trouble sleeping, anxiety, depression, tiredness and fatigue or bowel function disturbances that strike at the most inopportune moment? All of this and more, plus chronic stiffness, tenderness and agonizing pain in all your muscles, joints and tendons that teases, tortures and changes in location and intensity, like shifting sands, can be part of every day for the fibromyalgia sufferer.

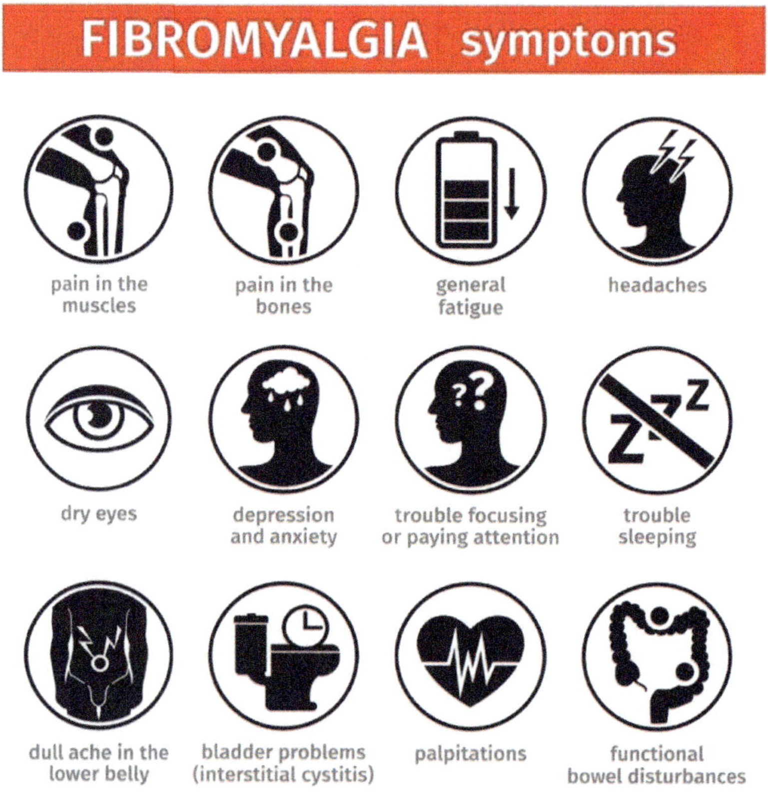

The above picture gives you a good idea of fibro symptoms, but it is not a complete list as everybody is different. Fibromyalgia is also called Fibromyalgia Syndrome (FMS).

2. Fascia

Fibromyalgia and fascia go together in my mind, but nobody else seems to mention them together.

The word Fascia originates from the Latin word Fascia, which means: "a band, bandage." In a fascia term environment, this is called a "sheath."

When I ask anybody if they know what fascia is, they reply: "*What is that? Never heard of it!*" It is difficult to explain fascia in non-medical terms, but I will give it my best shot.

You have probably heard someone saying: "*I have a huge knot in my neck!*" What they really mean is that they have tight fascia in their neck. Let me explain.

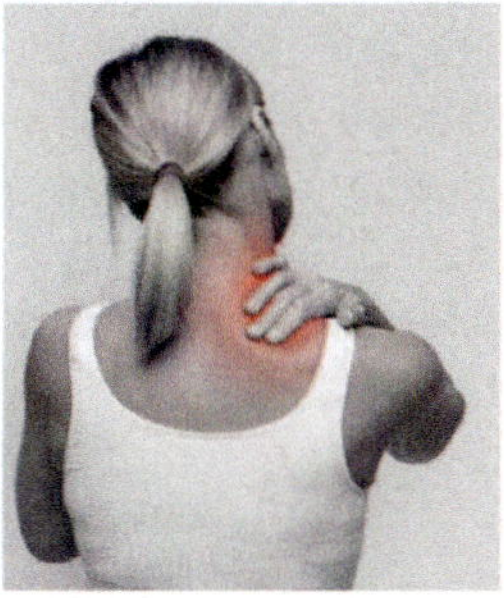

Fascia is a sheath of connective tissue covering your entire body (like a glove) from top to toe. Fascia surrounds and supports every blood vessel, nerve, muscle, bone, organ in your body. It is made up of different layers with liquid in between each layer for good lubrication so that each layer can slide over one another. Fascia holds everything together in your body. Without fascia/muscles, you would literally collapse on the floor and be a pile of bones.

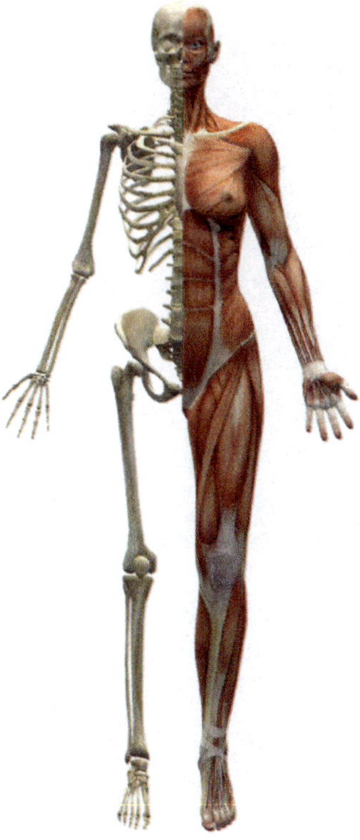

Fascia is designed to stretch as we move so all parts of our body must work together in harmony for optimum functioning. When you do any movement, your fascia needs to glide smoothly to do the movement. Your muscles need to be able to contract to do the movement, so the fascia needs to be able to stretch (as your muscle is surrounded by fascia), contract and relax. If the fascia is not smooth enough, so it is hard, sticky and thick, the muscle cannot contract properly resulting in limiting mobility and the creation of muscle knots (called fascia adhesions) in your body. **When fascia gets stiff, the sensory receptors get squashed, sending more pain signals to your brain.**

- Unhealthy fascia is tough, stiff, unbendable, dry, hard, matted, brittle and not supple at all.
- Healthy fascia is slippery, bendable, flexible, stretchable, gushy, elastic, soft and smooth.

You can see on this picture that when you run, all muscles work together and when the leg moves upwards, the calf muscles work too. When you move your arms, the chest muscles work too. If any of these muscles have unhealthy fascia in them, the other muscles will be affected too.

Important to watch: There is a brilliant video on YouTube ©. Search for: *"Fascia & The Mystery of Chronic Pain"* by Dana Sterling – a 12 minute video. You really must watch it to understand fascia.

a) Comparison with cling film

You can see on the picture below that the cling film is smooth and easy to stretch, like your fascia should be.

This picture tells a different story:

Here you can see that the fascia is no longer smooth. Once cling film (your fascia) is squashed together, it is extremely difficult to get it unwrinkled again. A very low heat iron might do the job. Hence why foam rolling (I will talk about this later) can be compared to "ironing out" tight fascia.

In a fibromyalgia patient, the fascia often feels and even looks (you can see the bumps in the muscles) like the cling film on the picture above: full of "pinched" cling film or in a fibromyalgia body: full of muscle knots.

Without treatment, the muscle knots can get so bad that another muscle tries to compensate by doing a job it is not designed to do, causing extra pain. The result can be muscle knots and compensating muscles all over your body causing severe pain. Fibromyalgia patients often describe their pain as: "pain all over my body".

Important note: Muscle knots are usually not the only problem in fibromyalgia patients as it is a complex condition.

b) Comparison with an orange
You can compare the fascia layers structure with an orange.

Fascia contains a lot of water, and the water sits in the different layers of the fascia. When you peel off the skin of an orange (this would be your skin) there is a thick white layer – this is your superficial fascia. If you peel that layer off, you will see that each segment of the orange has its own layers and wedges. If you carefully open these small wedges, there will be another layer of very small pockets that will have juice in. The human body is also packed with juicy wedges and layers.

However, in our body the juice looks more like gel rather than like water as it is mixed with other substances. The fascia is a vital lubricant in our body so that our muscles can glide fluidly next to one another as we move.

If you would squeeze out all the juice from the orange, it will become all sticky and almost impossible to pull the different layers apart. The same applies to your fascia.

c) The 4 main layers of fascia in your body
Fascia looks like one large sheet of tissue, but it has multiple layers:

- **Superficial fascia** is located immediately under your skin, all over your body.
- **Deep fascia** covers muscles, bones and nerves.
- **Visceral fascia** surrounds organs including stomach, heart and lungs.
- **Parietal fascia** which can be found in the lining of some body cavities e.g. around the pelvis.

Superficial fascia is the only fascia that you can feel when you touch your skin. To reach the other layers, you need to go much deeper. That's why there are deep-tissue massage treatments and "fascia tools" available (see further in this book).

d) The importance of water for healthy fascia

Our body is made up of approx.70% water. That water also sits in fascia. When you don't drink enough water, fascia gets too tight and no longer slides smoothly. Fascia is like a sponge and acts like a water reservoir for the body. If you neglect what your body needs (in this case water) your body will complain. Compare it to a car that hasn't been oiled for years; it won't drive very well at all. Your body cannot function without pain if your fascia is not healthy.

Fascia, for optimal performance and to avoid pains, needs to be:

- **Elastic** e.g. when we jump it needs to expand.
- **Stretchy** e.g. when we spread out an arm, the fascia needs to stretch and when this becomes too tight, dry or inflexible it can cause muscle knots and chronic pain that is often associated with fibromyalgia.
- **Moist and gliding** for even the smallest movement we make.
- **Healthy** for the refinement of our sensory receptors e.g. for our body awareness. Our sensory receptors lie within our fascia and they are nerve endings that send signals to our central nervous system. Fascia is our largest sensory organ as it has a very large surface area with sensory nerve endings.

You must be hydrated to have healthy fascia. If your urine is dark yellow, you are not drinking enough water. It needs to be light yellow.

e) Misdiagnosed chronic pain

Fascia has been overlooked for a long time although it holds our body together. Despite the major role fascia plays in every move that we make, many years ago, surgeons thought that fascia was "just" covering our organs and they just used to cut through the skin subsequently cutting through the fascia. Now they know that fascia surrounds nerves and nerve endings and just by cutting open the body, the fascia is affected, in a bad way. This is the reason why surgeons now use less invasive methods to operate and/or diagnose e.g. keyhole surgeries, endoscopy.

The first international "Fascia Research Congress" was held in Boston in October 2007. Before that, nobody, except for some specialists, knew about fascia and all its important functions. After the congress, people from all over the world realized that further research urgently needed to be done.

The medical field now starts to realize how important fascia is and how it can create chronic pain. Medical professionals who received their degree over 10 years ago haven't studied a lot about fascia and therefore many ignore related symptoms and possible treatments. This is also the reason why lots of chronic pain is misdiagnosed and pain killers are prescribed whilst often the pain is caused by fascia problems and muscle knots.

A lot of operations are done without being necessary. People have lower back operations only to find out that the pain didn't disappear and often even got worse. The potential reason for this: the **root** cause of the problem was never solved: **Fascia!** Of course, I realize that some conditions **do** need an operation to cure the pain but often creating healthy fascia can heal a lot of pain problems, without an operation. Always check with your medical professional to see **exactly** what the cause of your pain is.

A chronic pain specialist told me that if you have a medically unexplained chronic pain, the solution always lies in one of these:

- Stretch the muscle
- Mobilize the joint
- Glide the fascia

f) Proprioception

Proprioception is used in every movement that you make. It is your body's capability to sense action, location and movement, to know where you are in space. The sensory receptors (see point g) below), are in your joints, tendons, muscles and fascia, and they give signals to your nervous system and body for optimal proprioception. Examples of good proprioception:

- You know if your feet are standing on grass or on a concrete floor.
- You know if somebody puts 2 fingers on your back or a whole hand.
- You can open a door without having to look at your hand or arm.

If you have balancing problems or if you are constantly dropping objects or spill drinks, it could be that your proprioception is not as it should be. Proprioception can be trained.

g) Receptors
InNERvate (note part of the word "nerve") means "to supply nerves to". It also means "to supply with energy" or "to stimulate". You could say that innervate is "put the nerves into". When nerves go into muscle fiber, they innervate the muscle fiber. Our central nervous system receives the most sensory input from myofascial tissues.

Sensory nerves innervate the fascia tissue, called fascia innervation. The deep fascia is innervated with several different sensory receptors.

I know, I did say I wouldn't use technical mumbo jumbo in this book, but the next paragraph contains some, in order for me to get to the "easily bored receptor" which is an important receptor.

Some of the sensory receptors are mechanoreceptors, photoreceptors, thermoreceptors, proprioceptors and nociceptors, sometimes collectively called the Fascial Mechanoreceptors. Studies have shown that stimulation of these receptors makes changes in the nervous system. A slow deep tissue massage (manual pressure) produces parasympathetic reflex response and results in the person being more relaxed. There are Ruffini receptors, Olgi receptors, Pacini receptors and Interstitial receptors, just to name a few but it is beyond the scope of this book to explain all of these.

The easily bored receptor
There is one particular receptor I do want to talk about in more detail and these are the easily bored Interstitial receptors. This large group of receptors make up the majority of sensory input from fascia. The most important role of the receptors is to let you know the state of your internal environment or in other words how you are doing in general. When these receptors get bored – and they get bored very quickly – they change their job causing problems and pain. Daniela Meinl (founder of Integral Fascial Yoga) explained this very well during a presentation which I summarize below.

These receptors are like reporters of a very bad tabloid press. If there is something interesting to tell, they will write about it. If there is nothing interesting going on to tell the press, they make a drama out of nothing. The interstitial receptor have the same "attitude": if due to immobilization of muscles and nothing interesting is happening, they will change their threshold of stimulation with the result being that every stimulation that comes in will be interpreted as pain. That is a BIG problem.

If people are in pain, they stop moving because it hurts although not moving created the pain in the first place. It becomes a vicious circle that is extremely difficult to break. People have to do movements that are associated with proprioception so not just move but noticing how it feels when you move.

When you have myofascial pain, your proprioception in the area is reduced. The "2-finger test" is an example of this. Put 2 fingers on the back of a healthy person (without myofascial pain I mean) and that person will be able to distinguish that there are 2 fingers (fingers shouldn't be very close together though). When the 2-finger test is done on a person with myofascial back pain, the person would say: *"I am not sure if it is 1 finger of 2 fingers, I can't tell at all"*. The reason for this is because their proprioception is dramatically decreased.

Now the very **interesting** thing is that if you train the proprioception of the people who couldn't answer 1 or 2 fingers, their pain disappears! This could explain a lot of unspecific back pain. When you increase proprioception, you are inviting those receptors to take on their original job again, being a proprioceptor, rather than talking about everything, like the press does if there is no important news.

"Lower back pain is associated with decreased proprioception."
~ V. Leinonen ~

Daniela Meinl wrote a book titled: *"The comprehensive guide on fascial yoga. How to optimize the stimulation of fascia in your yoga practice."* If you want to dig deeper into fascial yoga I recommend reading this book.

Daniela is also a contributor to the "Fascia Training Academy", specialized in the latest research on fascia.

h) Barcelona airport

An interesting study was done in an airport in Barcelona. After a 10-hour flight, the passengers had to pick up their suitcases approx. 10 meters (or 10.9 yards) from the exit door of the plane. Result: most of the passengers had lower back pain when they lifted their baggage.

The people carrying out the study were curious what would happen when the passengers had to walk 100 meters (109 yards) to get to their baggage. Result: none of them complained of back pain.
Why is that?
When fascia is not used for a long period of time – 10 hours on the plane – the fascia degenerates, gets sticky and doesn't glide. This means when you lift a heavy object, after the surrounding muscles you need to

use to do the lifting have been immobilized for too long, those muscles will give you pain. The fascia needs to "wake up" first and get elastic, stretchy and be able to glide smoothly.

If the passengers who walked only 10 meters would have done some general body stretches or walked further, before grabbing their luggage, they would not have had back pain.

i) Pain cause by sudden movement
Visualize this scenario: You are in the kitchen, and you drop a knife. Your toddler is coming towards you so you bend down as quickly as you can and pick up the knife. "Ow" is your reaction because your back hurts.

The next day your back still hurts and you go to the doctor and say: "*It all started when I picked up a knife.*" You are convinced that bending down is the cause of the pain. You were wrong!

What you didn't consider is that you were sitting for 8 hours in your office before you went to the kitchen. The day before you also sat for 8 hours and the day before that too…

Your body wants you to be happy and will make sure that you can do all the movements you want to do. On the other side of the coin your body is controlled by your brain and your brain thinks like this: "*I am not going to look after the muscles you never use. If you want to sit for 8 hours every day, I will arrange things for you so you will be able to do that but don't ask me to look after the fascia in the immobilized area as I can't do that because fascia needs to move.*"

The cause of the pain when picking up the knife was not the bending down action BUT the cause was you sitting for too long so the fascia became stiff so can't do sudden movements without pain.

This is also the reason why fitness/dance/yoga classes etc. always start with a warm-up session. **Remember**: if you go from being non-active to active: always stretch first to avoid pain or move your body in different directions. Fascia doesn't like fast movements so whilst you have fibro pains: move slowly.

j) Your nervous system and fascia
Your fascial network influences your nervous system. There are many different nervous systems in your body but I will limit to talk only about the 3 listed below.

Autonomic Nervous System

- You **can't** control this system.
- It controls body parts and functions like heart, digestion, respiration, pupillary response urination and sexual arousal. This nervous system works and does its job unconsciously.
- It is a division of the peripheral nervous system that supplies muscles and glands, so influences the function of internal organs.
- It is regulated in the brain by the hypothalamus.

Sympathetic Nervous System

- You **can** control this system.
- It controls your "Fight or Flight" System. This prepares the body for stressful, dangerous or emergency situations. It also corresponds with arousal, energy generation and inhibits digestion.
- It is a system for actions that require a quick response.
- You can control this by calming your mind, do meditation, spend time in nature, have massages, etc. Shortly said: find ways to calm down your mind.

Parasympathetic Nervous System

- You **can** control this system.
- Chronic anxiety and stress play a very big role in over activating this system.
- Restores the body to be calm and turns off the stress reaction after a stressful situation.
- Your chillout system: promotes a "Rest and Digest" response, calming of the nerves to return to regular function and enhancing digestion. This can be done by mild exercises and deep breathing.

In many cases, both of these symptoms have "opposite" actions where one system activates a psychological response and the other inhibits it.

Some professionals say that fibromyalgia is caused by over stimulation of the sympathetic nervous system. Here is an analogy: the sympathetic system is the accelerator, and the parasympathetic system is the brake. These 2 parts should be talking to each other but in many cases they are not and they are out of balance, causing mental and physical problems. Your fascia will be badly influenced too. Remember: try and control your sympathetic and parasympathetic nervous system by keeping calm as much as possible.

3. Myofascial Pain

Use it or lose it! Lose your muscles or lose your movements! (and create pain).

The myofascial system (remember myo means muscle, fascia means sheath) of our body means that our muscles and our fascia work together as a unit. Fascia has nerves which makes it very sensitive.

When the fascia becomes dry and is not gliding anymore, the muscles cannot operate smoothly, and this causes myofascial pain: a chronic condition affecting fascia and muscles. This is where the term "myofascial release" comes from which I will talk about more later.

Muscle knots start to form because nothing is gliding properly. Muscle knots are very tense muscle fibers that stop your muscles from making certain movements without pain. These muscle knots need to be "ironed out" so they become smooth again. This can be done with myofascial release tools which you use on your body to remove the "sticky part" of the fascia. When the sticky water/gel disappears, it will be replaced by our body with fresh water, making functionality normal again and the pain disappears.

Some experts say that up to 85% of the general population will have myofascial pain at some time in their lives, making it a common syndrome.

Myofascial pain = unhealthy fascia.

Sometimes people confuse fibromyalgia with myofascial syndrome although they are 2 different conditions. Some specialists believe that muscle knots can lead to fibromyalgia. Others say that fibromyalgia can lead to muscle knots.

In my experience, muscle knots or myofascial pain is the **root cause** for the horrible pain all-over-your-body syndrome: fibromyalgia. It doesn't matter if the muscle knots were created physically or as a result of having tense muscles due to mental stresses.

When I was in unbearable pain, I had very unhealthy fascia and I was covered in muscle knots from top to toe and the more muscle knots you have, the worse the condition gets. Every tiny movement I made was painful. I changed my life, physically and mentally, consequently I changed my fascia resulting in no more pain. That sounds simple but that is what happened to me or let me re-word that: that is what I did to make it happen.

a) The main causes of myofascial pain

The main causes are:

- Immobilization is the biggest cause. Not moving enough!
- Inactivity or immobilization of a muscle or muscle groups which results in muscle weakness. This inactivity can cause a lot more damage to your muscles than over-use of muscles.
- Injury/accidents: banging into a wall will cause micro traumas in fascia and then cause restrictions.
- Many autoimmune diseases in which the body's own immunity negatively affects the different organ systems.
- Mood disorders
- Muscle injury
- Not drinking enough water (remember your body is appr. 70% water)
- Not moving enough in every-day life
- Over-work
- Poor posture for a long period of time e.g. hunching over a laptop or a mobile phone for hours without a break which means you are sitting in a position that is not in line with the natural curves of your spine.
- Repetitive movements causing muscle fatigue due to over-use
- Sitting too much
- Sleep disorders with results in constant fatigue
- Surgery and scar tissues. Scar tissue has to fill the hole created from the surgery and that skin that formed is more solid than other tissues around it, which can cause pain.
- Too much stress
- Trauma

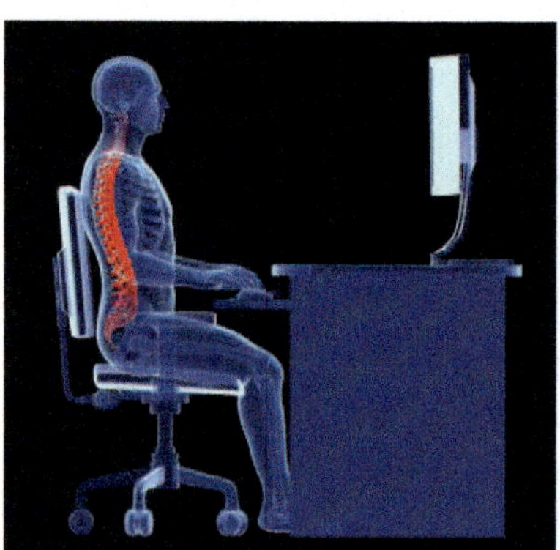

Correct position

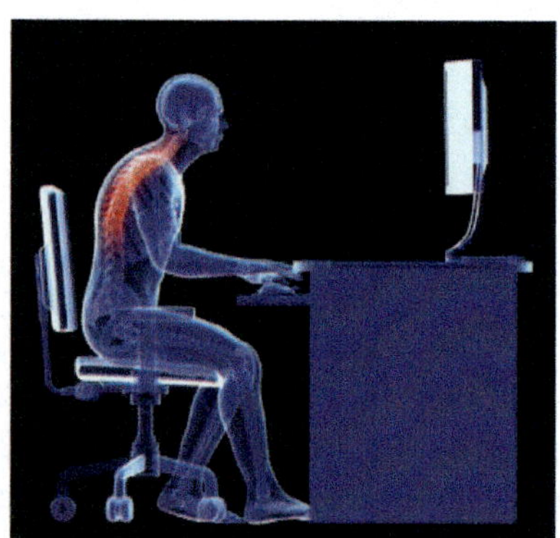

Incorrect position not in line with spine

b) Fascia is our largest sensory organ!
Are you ready for a shock? I know I was in shock when I learned about our largest sensory organ. It is truly unbelievable, I think.

Studies have shown that fascia is our largest sensory organ, with over more than 250 million sensory receptors in the fascia net. A lot of these receptors are located just under the skin but they are in the fascia of the entire body. Fascia contains more pain receptors than muscles and forwards signals to the brain constantly. Fascia is also closely linked to your autonomic nervous system.

Your body gives your brain information on how everything is going: there are sensory receptors for movement, pain, temperature, etc. A lot of the nerve endings are stretch receptors so we need to activate them. That's why stretches are very important to do and your body can feel much better after.

Martin Grunwald, a German Neurophysiologist, calculated that we have approx. 12 kilos (26 Pounds)!!!!! of receptors in our body. Yes, you did read that right: 12 kilos! The highest density of these receptors is between the muscles in the sliding layer.

I believe it is not difficult to understand, with so many sensory receptors in our body, why our nervous system is also affected by unhealthy fascia.

c) Stress is your worst enemy!
We all have stress in every-day life. Too much stress starts to give you physical symptoms and pain e.g. stomach upsets, tension in your head, feeling of not being able to cope, panic attacks, fatigue, stiff muscles, etc. When your level of stress gives you any of these symptoms: do something! Stop and analyze what you could possibly do to reduce some stress in your life. Stress is your worst enemy!

When you are free from fibromyalgia pain, stress can be a trigger to give you a flare up. Avoid stress as much as you possibly can. Don't get annoyed with silly things. Life is simply too short!

"It's not stress that kills us; it is our reaction to it!"
~ Hans Selye ~

"In the middle of difficulties lies opportunity."
~ Albert Einstein~

d) Move!
Avoiding everything from the above list of the main causes is not enough to have healthy fascia: you need to **move.** Your body is made to move and will not be happy when you sit for 4 hours without a break. If you do this, the fascia gets "crumbled up" and instead of being smooth gliding fascia for easy movements, the fascia becomes sticky and dry, sort of like a spider web.

So: **move!** Go for a walk, do some stretches, go for another walk, do more stretches, join a gentle fitness class or dancing lessons. Going to the gym does **not** solve sticky fascia. You don't have to get all sweaty to move. **YOU JUST NEED TO MOVE!**

MOVE your body = MOVE your fascia!!!

Tight fascia pulls everything out of alignment. If you pull on one side of cling film, the whole sheet of cling film will move. The same happens when you pull on a body part e.g. your arm, your whole fascia (from top to toe) will move too. You could also visualize a spider web to understand how fascia behaves: pull or push one side of the web and the whole web moves.

The World Health Organization (WHO) asserts that physical inactivity is now the fourth cause of death globally. "*Sitting will kill you*" was a newspaper headline not so long ago. We have all managed to adapt to a self-destructive lifestyle: a daily routine with hardly **any** physical movement!

e) Symptoms of unhealthy fascia (or myofascial pain)
The pain can vary from dull to constant to excruciating and everything else in between. The main symptoms are:

- A feeling that your muscles are weak
- Balance problems
- Constant fatigue
- Feeling depressed
- Feeling of having sore muscles
- Irritable Bowel Syndrome
- Limited motions in certain movements e.g. you can't move your arm up completely or you can't do your bra up with your hands on your back.
- Muscle pain that worsens or persists
- Numbness
- Poor sleep

- Referred pain: you lightly push one point on your skin anywhere on your body and you feel the pain further down or up in seemingly unrelated parts of your body.
- Severe muscle pain
- Tender muscles to touch
- Small nodules or bumps that are painful, even when you don't touch them. These nodules are sometimes visible on your skin.

Symptom: Tight muscles = tight fascia = muscle knots are formed.
Action: Release knots = release stuck fascia = release pain.

Myofascial Lines
I haven't spoken about Myofascial Lines in this book. These are lines of connective tissue in your body. Studying these lines can help you understand structural weaknesses in your body. A few examples of these lines: Superficial Back Line, Superficial Front Line, Lateral Line, Spiral Line, etc.

If you want to expand your knowledge about fascia and dive deep into Myofascial Lines and understanding of musculoskeletal anatomy, I recommend reading this book: "*Anatomy Trains*" by Thomas W. Myers. It is written for movement professionals and manual therapist so be prepared to see a lot of medical terminology.

f) How old do you think you are?
I have spoken to countless people who told me: "*I just can't do it anymore. I am too old!*". My husband used to tell me: "*You should work less, you are not 30 anymore!*". Where am I going with this? Well, I am talking about your body: your body is, by nature, not able to do the same things that you did 20 years ago. If you ever think you are getting too old for something: **stop** doing it. If not, your mind gets stressed, your muscles get stressed too and pain is coming your way.

Always remember that your mind usually feels younger than your body e.g. you feel like you are 30 but you are actually 50. Your muscles deteriorate as you get older: you lose muscle strength and muscle function. After the age of 30 your muscle mass decreases with approx. 8% per decade! Act your age and don't strain your muscles too hard or muscle knots are coming your way too.

g) Easing myofascial pain
I have tried countless creams, lotions, pads, etc. to easy my pain. I found these to work best for me:

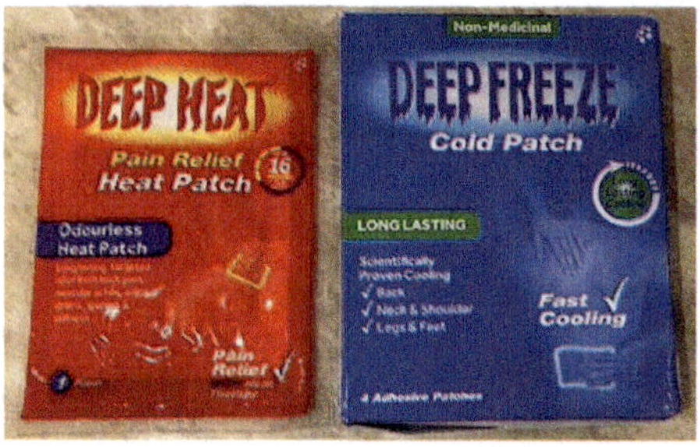

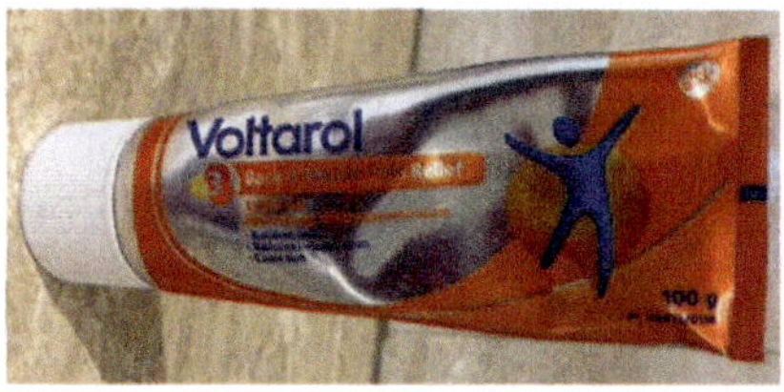

Important note: Fascia loves heat and nerves love cold. Most fibromyalgia sufferers will need both cold (sprays, cold shower, feet in cold water, etc.) and warm therapies (bath, sun, heating pads, etc.), definitely at the beginning of their recovery journey. You will soon know the difference between a nerve pain or a muscle pain. Nerve pain is tingling, sharp and stabbing whilst muscle pain is constant and dull although the pain can be excruciating in fibro sufferers rather than dull.

4. Myofascial Release

First you need to know what trigger points and referral pains are before you can do a release with a myofascial release tool.

a) Trigger points

Trigger points are tight bands in the fascia that have a knot in the middle. The most prone areas for myofascial trigger points are the neck, shoulders, lower back, buttocks, middle back, thighs, and calves.

Some people call trigger points "ouch" points and just pressing on the point elicits pain (people with fibromyalgia understand this all too well). Trigger points can cause weakness and pain in associated structures leading to associated nerve pain. Deep tissue massage therapists, athletic trainers, acupressure practitioners and chiropractors have identified referred pain patterns from the location of one trigger point.

Sticky fascia and contracted muscle cells can create a painful lump or hot spot called a trigger point and these are very common in people with fibromyalgia. Focusing on treating those trigger points can reduce local muscle pain. The most effective treatments to get rid of these local muscle pains involve physically disrupting the tissue by stretching, massage and rolling. On this picture you can see the most common trigger points.

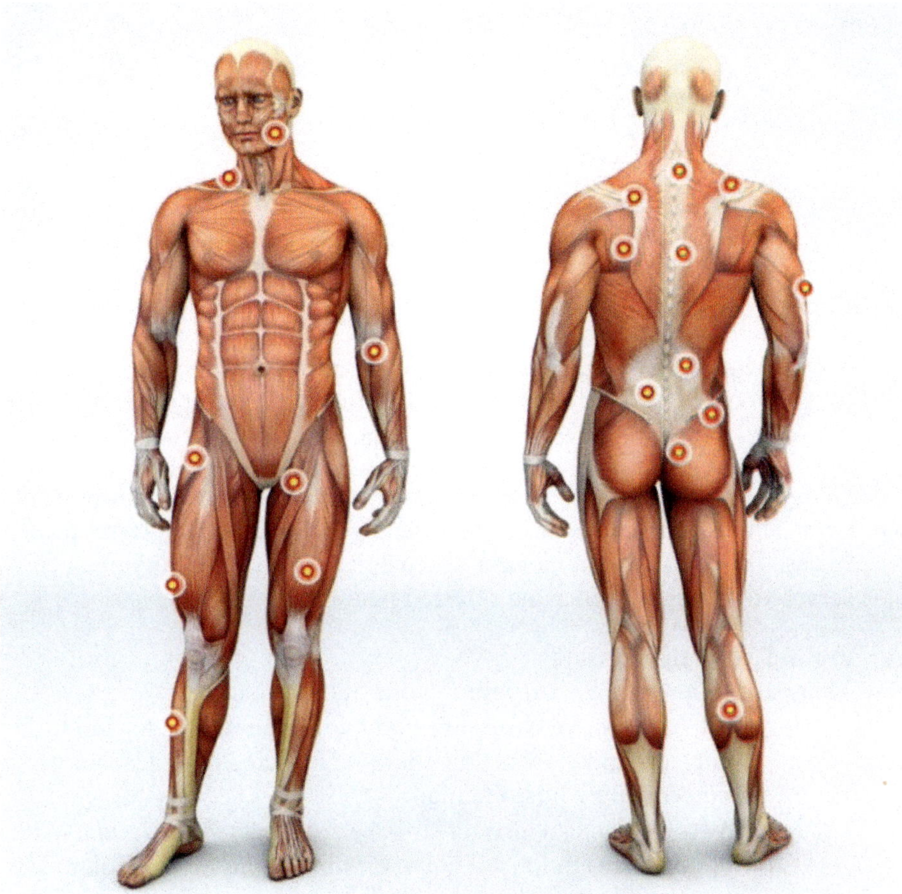

b) The pain area is often not the area to treat

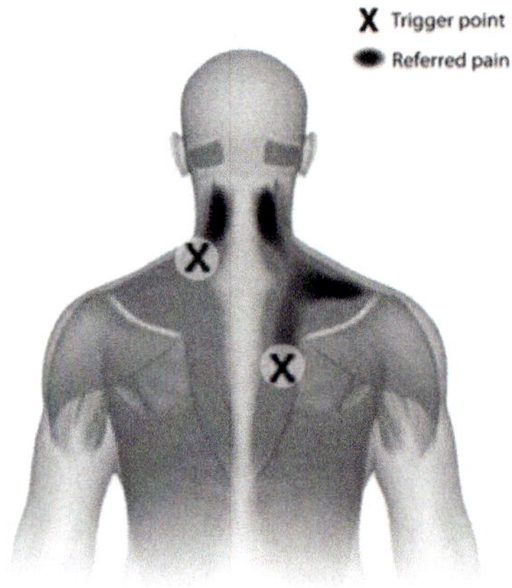

Often the area that is painful is **not** the area to treat with a myofascial release tool but where the "X" is on the drawing is the root problem of the pain. If you would treat the black area, you wouldn't solve the pain.

On www.triggerpoints.net you can find which trigger point causes your pain. This is an excellent website to help you understand referral pains. In case this website is no longer live when you read this book, just search for "trigger points and referred pain".

c) Find your tight fascia
There are different ways of finding your tight fascia:

- **Feel**. Just feel all over your body with your hands to find little bumps or tender areas that could be muscle knots. Use very mild pressure whilst feeling.
- **Stretch**. You can also do stretches to locate stuck fascia. When you do a side stretch as shown on the picture below, you might feel that certain areas feel "tight" and give you a tiny bit of discomfort whilst stretching. You can, of course, find stiff areas in any other stretch too, not just with a side stretch.

Roll on a foam roller or a ball (explained in the next few pages) on these tight areas and do the stretch again and the tight area might now feel completely normal. That's how easy release can be.

It is always good to stretch again after you have used any myofascial release tool e.g. if you have released a knot in your calf, stretch your calf for 20 to 30 seconds.

d) Foam roller

The foam roller is generally considered to be very effective for releasing tight fascia and relieving pain symptoms. You will find other release tools later in this book. Foam rollers improve moisture penetration and as a result the fascia is better lubricated. Muscle tension is relieved after foam rolling.

Price of foam rollers vary a lot; you can buy one for under $20 USD or £12 or $20 CAD. (Prices were correct at time of printing)

If you have no budget at all: you could fill a **very strong** plastic bottle with a bunch of old socks or an old T-shirt and use that for your fascia release. Make sure you test the strength of the bottle so there is no risk for you to get "plastic bits" stuck into your skin.

Important note: Foam rolling is not suitable for young people under 16 years old. The use of myofascial balls are more recommended for this age group.

Foam rollers come in different shapes and sizes: soft, medium soft, hard, spiky, grid and vibrating ones. I would recommend starting with a soft one if you have a lot of pain. You don't really need anything else but the simplest foam roller. These sizes are usually available:

- 12" or 30cm. You can use these to roll on one leg whilst leaving the leg you are not rolling next to you with foot on the floor, for stability.
- 18" or 46cm. These are ideal to roll over your shoulders and back.
- 36" or 90cm. You can use this roller for rolling the front of your thighs on both legs together.

There are 2 ways of foam rolling:

- **Fast rolling**: roll 6 to 8 times fast over the roller with a body part. The purpose of this type of rolling is to loosen the tissue and create better mobility range.
- **Slow rolling**: roll super slow over a body part. Sink into the roller and put your body weight on it, supporting yourself with your hands. Slow rolling is done to release muscle knots and to change the water content of the fascia. The goal is to break up the muscle knots and soften the tissue. An example of slow rolling: take minimum 3 minutes to roll your upper thigh from just above your knee to your groin. That's how slow! Hold (stop rolling) for 10 to 20 seconds when you feel a "tender area" and then roll further.

When foam rolling, practice proprioception as often as possible. This means to connect your brain to the muscles you are foam rolling by thinking about the muscle and visualizing that body part and muscle in your mind. Muscle knots will remain until the knotted area is broken by myofascial release.

How often do you do foam rolling?
Fast rolling: You can do fast rolling daily on different body parts. Don't press too hard though.

Slow rolling: only do one body part on any given day. Leave 48 hours in between before you do that same body part again, giving the muscles time to adjust. Don't do exercises or fitness training for 48 hours after slow rolling. For people over 60 years old: leave 72 hours between sessions as your body needs longer regeneration time.

Too hard and too long is never good for fascia release and could cause bruising or create the opposite effect.

e) Successful release

How do you know that whatever you are doing actually works? What does a release feel like? For most people a muscle knot release feels like: *"Aaaaaah that feels sooooo nice"*. Your body can sink into the muscle knot, and you feel it: a bump has gone under your skin. Sometimes you can feel a "clunk" feeling and you know something has changed in the fascia. This means you have successfully done a myofascial release.

Usually release feels satisfying and relaxing. It can feel like a good pain that your body needs. The body part you have released will move better, feel better and the pain is gone. The same principle applies when using balls for releases instead of a foam roller. Please note that the area you have released can be a little sore sometimes but that should not last longer than 24 hours.

You can use a foam roller for your whole body:

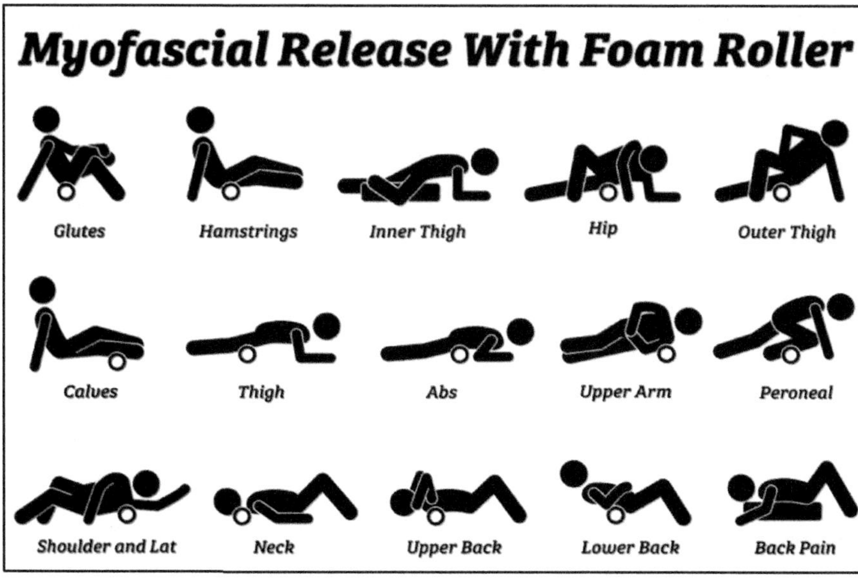

f) 6 steps for maximum success

Here are the 6 steps to take for maximum potential of releasing muscle knots. Let's say you are releasing your front upper thigh in this example.

1) Warm up your body/muscles by doing some gentle exercises or take a bath/shower or sit in the sun.
2) Practice proprioception (think about your thigh)
3) Do some fast rolling on your thigh to loosen up the tissue
4) Do some slow foam rolling on your thigh to release knots
5) Do some stretches for your thigh after foam rolling
6) Relax for a while, at least a few minutes.

There is actually a seventh step that you **could** do: strengthen the muscles. It is important to know though that all muscle knots need to be released (returning the muscle to its normal length) before you can strengthen the muscle. I suggest you search for: "strengthening exercises for thigh".

g) Important points for myofascial release

- **Very important: Drink a lot of water before and after you do myofascial release as you now know that the water in the thick fascia is replaced by our body with fresh water. If you don't drink, there is no fresh water for replacement and your fascia will not become wet so won't glide and the pain won't disappear.**
- Fully relax, let your body sink into the ball or foam roller and do deep-breathing whilst rolling.

- Whilst breathing, breathe into the body part you are releasing.
- Don't go beyond mild discomfort.
- Don't expect overnight results but be patient.
- Never do too much too hard or too long as this can create muscle/nerve damage.
- If you're pregnant, have varicose veins, inflammation, osteoporosis or other diagnosed conditions, speak to your healthcare provider before doing release.
- Listen to your body.
- Best results are obtained by rolling in the directions of the muscles.
- Stop immediately if you feel real pain. You will soon learn the difference between "a good pain" and real pain.
- Don't roll on these areas:
    - Neck (best left to professionals)
    - Breasts
    - Abdomen
    - Ribs
    - Bruised areas
    - Directly over a bone
    - Swollen or inflamed areas

h) The lazy way

Foam roller under lower back
Well of course I don't want to recommend the lazy way as you are not moving at all this way. However, next time you just want a little peace and rest; why not play some relaxing music and "just lie still" on a foam roller.

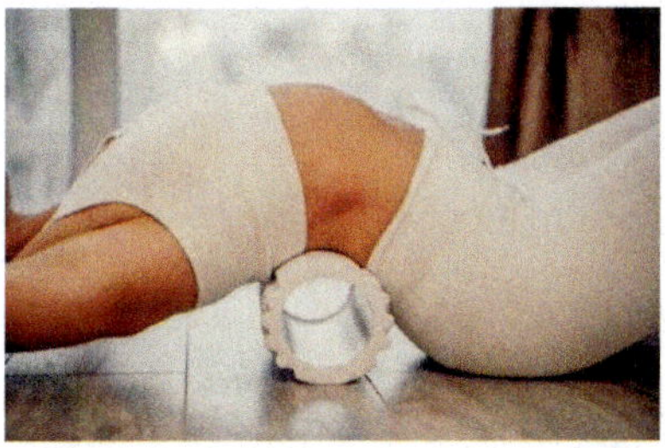

This lazy way shown above is very good for your lower back muscles (assuming you have no medical back conditions) and it stretches your chest muscles too. Start with only a few minutes and, assuming you don't have pain afterwards, next time do more minutes and work your way up to 20 minutes. Just pure relaxation. You will feel the difference when you get up! You can also use a bunch of pillows under your back instead of a foam roller.

Legs up the wall

OK, whilst we are talking about being lazy, here's a yoga pose I really like. It is called "legs-up-the-wall" yoga pose (I wonder why they called it that 😊). You can stay in this position for up to 20 minutes. Just relax and practice deep breathing and perhaps put some relaxing music on.

It is an inversion pose meaning that your upper body is in a different position from being upright. Here are the benefits:

- Can help with headaches
- Can help with sleep deprivation
- Heals mild anxiety
- Helps digestive issues
- Helps to manage stress
- Improves circulation
- It calms your body and mind
- It is very relaxing, activates the relaxation response in your body
- Stretches the back of your neck
- Stretches your legs; hamstrings and calves

Yin Yoga

I can't believe I am giving you a third lazy way, but Yin Yoga has great benefits for fascia and for your mind, so I really do have to mention it. In Yin Yoga, you do passive long-held poses for stretching to access the deeper layers of fascia and to calm your mind. These floor poses often focus on the lower part of your body: lower spine, hips, inner thigs and pelvis as these areas have a lot of connective tissues. You can hold the poses for between 5 and 20 minutes. Start with one minute and work your way up. Below are a few examples of poses. Search for "yin yoga poses" to find more.

Important note: when you practice Yin Yoga, only stretch 60% of your maximum stretch capability.

i) Weird but true

I've mentioned that stress sits in your body and in your fascia. By releasing the muscle knot created by stress, you also release negative emotions. On many occasions when I did foam rolling, I started to cry very unexpectedly the moment I felt a release in a muscle. Reason for the crying: the emotional stress was released! Isn't that just wonderful and amazing! Crying during release, in a way, is happy crying as it means release.

j) Do you do myofascial release forever?

Gosh no, you don't need to do myofascial release forever. I will try to explain this with a comparison to a light switch. Imagine you are trying to turn on a light switch, but you don't have the force in your hand to be able to do this. You try again and again and again but the light doesn't switch on. You can try for an hour but if the force is not enough, nothing will happen. You do some hand exercises to increase your strength. You **can** now turn the light switch on! When the light is on, it stays on.

That's exactly how fascia works. You have to do myofascial release and stimulate your fascia until you have the effect where the switch stays on. Once the area you release no longer causes you pain or problems, you don't need to do release over and over again as the message has been transmitted to the brain that release has happened and no more pain signals will be sent to your brain. You **could** do a few repetitions every few weeks on that body area you released, as a preventative measure, but you certainly don't need to do it over and over again.

When the light is on, it stays on; when the fascia is healthy, it stays healthy but **only** if you have also changed your lifestyle and don't repeat the unhealthy things that caused your pain. If you do that, your hand to switch on the light is weaker again so the muscle you released becomes weaker again too.

5. The Importance of Stretching

Let's have a quick look at the picture below.

By sitting in this position some muscles are shortened and others are lengthened.

Shortened muscles:

- Your groin - sitting in this position
- The front of your neck – looking down
- Your hip flexors (muscles towards front of your hips)
- Your chest muscles – hunching down

Lengthened muscles:

- Your upper back – rounded shoulders
- Your shoulders – rounded shoulders
- The back of your neck – head forwards

Immobilized muscles:

- Your hamstrings (back of upper thighs)
- Your buttock muscles
- Your hips

When there is a shortened area in your body, there is also a lengthened area so there is no muscle balance in the relevant muscle groups. These are called underactive and overactive muscles.

Tight hamstrings and tight hip flexors can cause back pain because the fascia will be pulling all over the place. Chronically shortened muscles can create muscle knots. By sitting in a hunched over position the fascia in your back, shoulders and neck will have to adjust and change and will become tight. This chronic shortening can create muscle knots.

By doing stretches, you are stretching your fascia in all directions which is important for healthy fascia. The gentle movement of your fascia will restore some sticky areas to a more fluid state. You hold a stretch for anything between 1 and 2 minutes. During the stretch, you might feel some parts of your body are more stiff than other parts. It is those parts **you need to move more.**

If you hold a stretch for longer than 90 seconds, you are targeting the deeper fascia layers.

You might not always have time to stretch 1 or 2 minutes but even holding stretches for a few seconds is better than no stretching at all.

Can you see how in the picture above your organs are constantly squashed in this position? This can result in digestive problems and can cause stomach pain.

The rib cage is also squashed and cannot expand properly. Subsequently this will impact oxygen flow in your body and that will have an impact on your breathing. The strain on the neck and back is huge and the strain will travel to your head, causing headaches.

When there are a **lot** of muscle knots in one body area e.g. leg, you won't be able to stretch them out. You will have to "iron out" the muscle knots before doing the stretches afterwards.

In the picture below you can see that lots of muscles in your leg are inter-connected (ignore the Latin names). This means that when one muscle isn't functioning optimally, the other movements required with any of the other muscles might cause pain. You can imagine that all those muscles will pull on your hip causing hip pain.

Note that there is one large muscle which attaches to the spine in your lower back (the muscle on top of the picture). This is the psoas muscle also called the "stress muscle." Now imagine again that the muscles in your legs ***and*** in the psoas muscle are pulling on your hip and your back. Do you see how this can cause tightness, tenderness, discomfort and back pain? I hope the answer is yes. A tight psoas muscle can give you pain in seemingly unrelated aches in your leg, hip, lower back, bladder and pelvis.

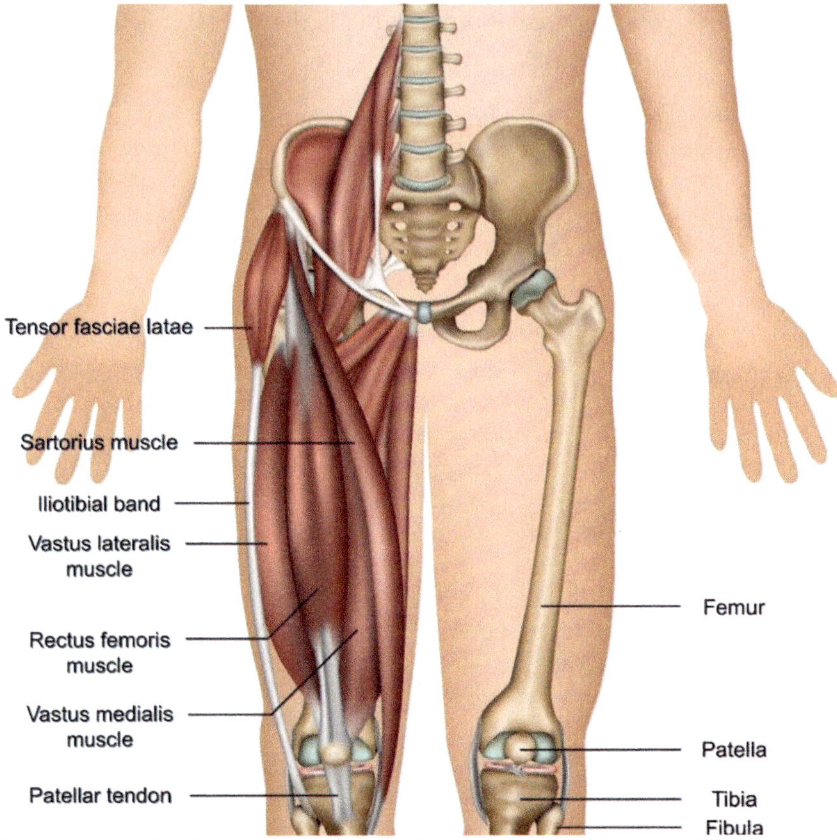

Whatever profession you are in or whatever you do in your life: pay attention to your muscles and try and analyze which ones are shortened or lengthened for too long. You know what to do: stretch them.

a) How do you stretch?

Stretch in the opposite way of the shortened muscles e.g. for the hunched sitting position you need to stretch your groin, the front of your neck, your hip and your chest muscles. The lengthened muscles: upper back, shoulders and back of neck, need to shorten. This stretch does all that:

Below are some other gentle stretches you could do.

Listen to your body when you do stretches. Your body will tell you what area isn't in optimal state and where you need to stretch the most. It's always a good idea to rotate your body whilst you are in a stretch, whatever stretch you do, as we don't do many rotations with our body in every-day-life. After a few stretches, you will know how good you feel afterwards, and you will want to do more. Make sure to hold onto something if you do stretches that are challenging for your balance.

Some stretches and exercises if you sit on the computer too much:

Some neck stretches if you sit on the computer too much:

Never over-stretch.
Just stretch to the point of a "light" pull.
You should never have pain whilst stretching.

How often do you do stretches?

Whenever and wherever you are standing or sitting and not doing anything: stretch or move your body by moving it slowly in all sorts of directions or march on the spot or make circles with your hips, etc. Do anything as long as you move! I call these: on-the-spot Mini-stretches or Mini-Movements. You only need to stretch or move for a few seconds as a few seconds of movement is better than no movement. You could stretch your calves standing in a queue or move your feet left and right. You could stretch your arms whilst standing in the kitchen waiting for the kettle to boil. You could stretch your legs whilst sitting in a chair. You get the idea: stretch your fascia as much as you can whatever you are doing.

Instead of mini movements, you could do all sorts of stetches and movements, in longer sessions, on a regular basis e.g. every 2 or 3 days for 15 minutes but make sure you are doing gentle stretches.

Lastly, you could do stretches for 2 minutes in the morning and before you go to bed. Find what works best for you and decide when and how often to stretch and move. Your body will be your guide.

b) Act like a cat!
If you own a cat, you know that after each sleep, the cat will do a massive all-over-body stretch and yawn at the same time. It is called pandiculating. If you have ever seen a cat stretching by arching their back, you have seen a pandiculating response. The full stretch wakes up the muscles that have been inactive.

Maybe all the above methods of stretching are too much for you or you don't want to make the time to move more. In that case I suggest that you stretch like a cat, at least every day and especially when you wake up in the morning. It will not solve your fibro pain but at least you are moving and stretching a little bit.

You can also, should you feel like it, stretch like this cat☺:

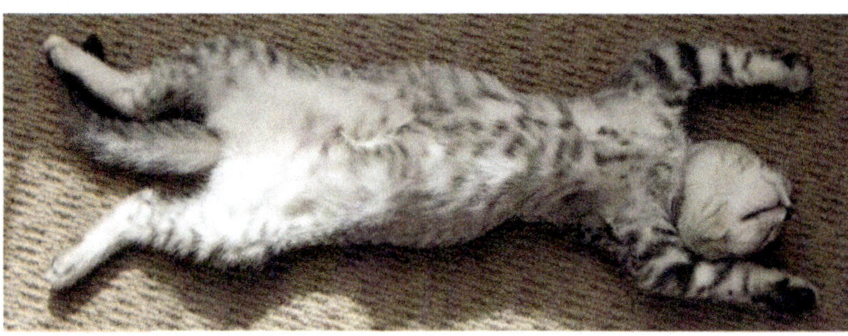

c) Children should do stretches
Today's children are already sitting in the wrong posture from a very young age. No doubt this will cause them problems when they get older. Tell your children to get up more often, do some stretches or move their body in several directions, at least every hour. You could put a timer on their phone or laptop to remind them to get up and move, even for a few movements.

"In the olden days" children used to play in the streets all day, climb trees, do a lot of sports, watch little or no TV, jump rope, walk more as not everybody had a car, play ball games, play with hoops, skipping ropes and marbles, etc. All the things that a body is designed to do to keep fascia healthy. Now they are on their computers and phones all day long! Is it any wonder that the population gets younger and younger to complain of muscle pains?

I predict a lot of fibromyalgia diagnoses when the children of today are adults, or even teenagers. My friend's 10-year-old daughter complained of neck pain every day. I told my friend to make her daughter practice some of the methods you are reading in this book and guess what: yep, her neck pain is gone! It **can** be that simple to solve pain.

Important note: There are no stretches that will heal your pain unless you also address the environment in which you are asking your body to heal. What I mean here is that if you stretch but don't change anything else in your lifestyle, the problems will just keep coming back over and over again.

Chapter 2: Mind-Body Connection

by Christine Clayfield

The Mind-Body connection was a very big eye-opener for me. The biggest ever! You can control your pain with your mind! You will note that "too much stress and anxiety" is listed in: "Main causes of myofascial pain" previously in this book. You've read that fascia is usually not the only problem with fibromyalgia. Another big problem: **your mind, your emotions.**

Like many of us, you might sometimes feel overwhelmed with everything daily life throws at you. Emotions like anger, sadness and fear can cause a feeling of stress. Fascia has an emotional memory as emotions "store up" in your fascia. Therefore negative emotions will affect the state of your fascia, the state of your pain. When stress becomes chronic stress, it will affect us physically and mentally. Myofascial release can help to "unstick" the fascia where these emotions are stored, to reduce the stress by releasing the areas of pain that correspond to difficult emotions to deal with.

You cannot physically heal completely if your mind is troubled and not calm and happy. Negative emotions totally lock up your body if you don't process them: anger, guilt fear, worry. It all translates into body tension and that tension is stored in your fascia. Your emotional state plays a very big role in how tight your body feels. Who would have thought? 😊 Remember:

Emotions are the missing link in your physical healing. Your physical body is simply an expression of your emotions.

Overthinking is a very big cause of unhappiness. Here are a few thoughts that might help you to stop overthinking:

- The problems is rarely the problem. The way you think about the problem is. 99% of your feelings are caused by you and your thoughts. 1% is caused by reality.
- Most problems are solved with less thinking about the problem. A lot of answers can be found in silence, with a clear mind or with a peaceful rest with your eyes closed. ***You see the light better when you close your eyes!***

- Acceptance is peace: Accept the now, accept the uncontrollable and the imperfections.
- Make peace with yesterday, let go of tomorrow and focus on **now**.
- Our health is not measured by how many times you go to the gym but true health is measured by the quality of your positive thoughts and the mind being in complete peace. Health starts in your mind.
- Never allow pain to destroy you. Instead, let it make you stronger.
- Most problems are not solved with more thinking, they are solved with less.
- Really LET GO of what is out of your control. Don't just say that you will do it. Move on.
- Find peace and everything will fall into place.

Your mind is inseparable from your body/muscle tension. Mental and physical conditioning in your body are linked: whatever affects the mind also effects the body and vice versa. Your body gets stiff if you are worried and have chronic stress and this creates tense muscles, muscle knots, therefore tense fascia. Stress is mostly stored in your hips, neck and shoulders.

It is unbelievable but true that you can stop your hip pain by doing certain hip stretches, myofascial release treatments and stress-meditation. You can go from chronic hip pain to total hip freedom without any operation!

You'll stay in your trauma forever unless you address where the trauma is stored in your body. The body remembers everything, and it hides away emotions that are not ready to be processed in your tissue. Myofascial release can release these tissue problems but only if you are ready to process your feelings. You can learn how to calm your mind whenever the world is crashing down on you! The medical field is starting to understand the mind-body connection in the light of chronic pain.

The more stressed or miserable you are, the more pain you will have. The more pain you have, the more stressed and miserable you are. Don't think about your pain all the time as it triggers the brain to start worrying and you can get potentially stuck in fight or flight mode – and stay in the fight mode! Don't obsess over little pains. Your anxiety will tell you the worst-case scenario. It's a liar; don't listen.

Anxiety affects your body which affects your emotions which affect your body and round and round it goes. When your mind is not relaxed and constantly busy analyzing all your pain you tell your brain you have, the body cannot concentrate on using it's own natural healing system and cure whatever is wrong. You will be surprized how much the body can heal with a calm and relaxed mind.

Learn to be happy with what you have. Nobody sells tickets to happiness. You must create it yourself: plant it and feed it to grow. Life is much easier when you are happy!

Re-train your brain and more healing will happen naturally.

Your sleep and your fascia

When we sleep, we go through different phases of sleep. During the deep sleep phase, your body works on healing. During this phase, you need a high distribution of HGH (Human Growth Hormone). This hormone keeps your fascia healthy and elastic. It makes sure that your fascia and your muscles are fully relaxed during sleep. If you don't sleep well, especially if you don't get enough deep sleep, your fascia will be really badly affected and become very sticky.

The good news

This all sounds pretty gloomy so far but the good news is that nearly every myofascial pain can be treated through self-treatment. You can re-model your fascia network with the right stimuli. Giv3 your fascia what it wants, and your fascia will give you a painless body.

"The greatest disability is in the mind, not the body!"
~ Stephen Hawking ~

Please remember the mind-body connection, as it is crucially important for your fibromyalgia recovery!

Note from author Victoria B. Allen: OK, now that Christine Clayfield has shared some of her knowledge, I hope you understand how important fascia and movement are in our body and how it can cause pain. Now I can tell you what **I** did to become pain free.

Chapter 3: The First Ouch & The Shifting Sands

The First Ouch

The first Ouch is about what happened to me before I realized that this was a warning about what was about to become the chronic condition known as fibromyalgia. My fibro story, although I was unaware of it at the time, began while I was relaxing in my favorite chair and was suddenly struck by an intense stabbing pain in my toe. This pain was so extreme that I jumped and screamed out loud *"Ouch! -- What was that!"* It literally felt like someone had just stabbed my toe with a sharp needle.

My husband looked at me like I'd just lost my mind and honestly, I was left wondering if I had imagined it, because as acute as this momentary pain was, it almost immediately vanished. Slowly, over the next few months, I continued to ignore these random occurrences of knife-like pain that would occur without warning, and never in the same place, until the simple act of walking a block or getting up and down from a chair caused pain in my joints, muscles and ligaments that had become too severe to ignore.

Being the self-sufficient, researching, problem-solving, A-type-personality that I am, I went on to the Internet to find a logical answer for these irrationally insidious and increasingly debilitating pains I was experiencing. At this point, my day was no longer simply ignoring a fleeting stabbing pain. I was now feeling irritable, frustrated and exhausted because the pain I was feeling had taken over my entire body, limiting my ability to sleep at night or even put on my own socks and tie up my shoes.

Over the course of a few months, my usually happy and active day had quickly turned into a bleak and brutal nightmare. Everything I was reading about Fibromyalgia, this nefarious syndrome of unknown origin, that apparently had no cure, left me feeling thoroughly depressed. Medical professionals couldn't explain my symptoms.

Not being someone who was used to feeling depressed, this was an entirely unexpected experience for me. I can tell you from personal experience that waking up one morning to find yourself in a position of having to deal with a daily life of pain can leave you feeling depressed in very short order.

When you've already got enough to worry about in your day, on top of everything else, how do you deal with feelings of depression? While there is so much that will be helpful in subsequent chapters, the starting point is to first acknowledge and identify your various pains.

The writing space below is for you to journal or write about your first Ouch! And all that followed, and how they made you feel.

Why? Because the simple act of seeing in writing what has caused you pain, and what feelings this evokes, is the first step toward removing the power that these fibro pains hold over you and gaining some insight into what you need to do to free yourself.

____

____

____

____

____

____

____

____

____

____

OK, now that you've taken some of your power back and acknowledged when you first noticed the signs of fibromyalgia and how it may have progressed for you, let's find out how we can get your life back to the way you want it to be.

The shifting sands

Fibromyalgia is like the shifting sands of the Sahara Desert in that the pains often associated with fibro are elusive and continually shifting from place to place. Like the camel, you need to learn how to navigate so that you can stay on course. One day it's an unexpected sharp pain in your toe, the next day it may be all your fingers are stiff for no reason, and the next, perhaps your hip joints are on fire and the simple act of standing up from a seated position has you shouting out your favorite swear words.

Fibromyalgia is devious, merciless and mercurial. It attacks everyone in their own special way, and in different degrees of intensity that vary from day to day. Then you begin to feel a little better and your energy is returning so you walk that extra block, and guess what? *"Bloody Hell!"*, what you thought was all better strikes back with a vengeance to say, *"Surprise! Fibro is not done with you, yet."*

These shifting pains can easily make any person feel like they're losing their mind. When there seems to be no explanation for why these shifting pains may be occurring, it can be so very difficult to understand what's happening to your body, let alone knowing what you should do about it.

When the mind is confused about what the body is saying, taking the appropriate action to deal with unpredictable pain can definitely be a challenge. However, this can also be an opportunity to learn how to be much more attuned to your body, how you navigate your world, and what life lessons you may still have left to be learned.

Some estimates report only 10% of men are affected by fibromyalgia. That means that lucky women make up the 90% of those tormented by this nefarious syndrome.

I've spent most of my life being proudly stubborn about toughing out pretty much anything – that is, until fibro taught me a better way. Being "tough" lead me down a path that I now realize most likely was, at least in part, the cause of my fibro pain. I had no problem working twice as hard, twice as long as everybody else I know, and I was even seeking out traditionally male-oriented roles to prove to the world that "I can do it all."

A-personality

Better late than never, so they say, and as I share my fibro experiences with you, it's patently obvious that while there are certainly benefits to every personality type, my previous lifestyle choices had locked me into an A-type personality.

What is an A-personality and why might this personality type contribute to being affected with fibro? A-personalities are people who are typically:

- Ambitious
- Competitive

- Goal-orientated
- Have a time urgency
- High achievers
- Highly organized
- Impatient
- People with strong work ethic
- People with tendency to constantly multitask
- Pro- active in their pursuits
- Workaholics

The strong drive for achievements and success that some of these A-personalities have makes them more prone to stress, anxiety and burnout and they have difficulties between balancing professional and personal lives. They often give priority to work rather than self-care and relaxation. These people seek their own "being-good-enough-feelings" by their achievements and they feel like they are "not good enough" compared to others unless they are succeeding in their goals.

While these traits are often beneficial for career success, what's the point if there is no room to enjoy life along the way? Although I recognized my A-personality traits long ago, I did not realize that they were likely going to contribute to increased risk of health problems at some later point in my life.

I also realized long ago that I developed these traits early in my childhood because of trying to please an angry, military-like father who was never pleased with anything. Still, all these long years later, understanding the whys and wherefores was not enough to protect me from racing headlong through my A-personality life until I came face to face with fibromyalgia. In other words, strange as it may seem, I really have to say, *"Thanks, Fibro"* because without your painful lessons I would never have learned to slow down, ditch the stress and guilt, enjoy every day, take a breath, take a holiday, and be the person I was truly meant to be.

If you tend toward being an A-type-personality, perhaps reading this book will motivate you to re-write your story and help you to be kinder to yourself.

If you find that my favorite mantra, which you will find at the end of each chapter, brings a smile and helps you to feel enthusiastic and empowered, please make it your own:

"Wake up – Kick Ass – Repeat"

Chapter 4: Hidden Dangers

Fibromyalgia comes with many hidden dangers. There are many obvious dangers in the world that can adversely affect your physical and mental health that we all need to be aware of as we travel through our lives. We are taught as children to be careful around things that can harm us, and for the most part, this is fairly easy to do.

However, have you ever stopped to consider that there may be just as many hidden dangers in your daily world that may not be as easily identified, yet can still cause great harm to your mind and body?

OK, you're starting to say to yourself, *"What on earth is she rambling on about?"* I hear you, and don't worry, it's not something out of this world, like aliens or sasquatch sightings.

This chapter is simply about those things in our day-to-day environment that we have grown to believe, such as opinions that may not actually be true. This would include environmental concerns, that while invisible to the eye, are causing much greater harm than most would realize. Your very thoughts can create your own unhealthy reality.

We live in a world in which we stop asking questions and seeking answers to the obscure or currently unknowable. As Confucius so aptly reminds us:

"The one who knows all the answers has not been asked all the questions."
~ Confucius ~

1. The Medical Opinion

Most of us have grown up to believe, without question, that whatever the traditional medical model tells us must be true. I consider this to be one of the hidden dangers. While nobody really seems to definitively understand this elusive fibromyalgia condition, the medical professionals still have much to say about it. The Mayo Clinic describes the condition as:

"...a disorder characterized by widespread musculoskeletal pain accompanied by fatigue, sleep, memory and mood issues."

Researchers believe that the way your spinal cord and brain processes pain signals is amplified by fibromyalgia resulting in more painful sensations. Many clinics and medical resources are not exactly encouraging or hopeful in their diagnosis, as evidenced by their various opinions and diagnoses, as follows:

Mayo Clinic: *"While there is no cure for fibromyalgia, a variety of medications can help control symptoms."*

Johns Hopkins: *"The cause is unknown. There is no cure for fibromyalgia, but symptoms can be managed."*

Cedars-Sinai: *"The cause is unknown. There are no tests that can confirm a diagnosis of fibromyalgia. There is no known cure for fibromyalgia, but symptoms can be managed."*

National Institute of Health: *"The cause of fibromyalgia is not known. There is no cure for fibromyalgia, but doctors and other health care providers can help manage and treat the symptoms."*

Why wouldn't receiving such a hopeless diagnosis make you feel even more anxious or depressed? If you believe it, of course it might. Personally, I find it quite perplexing that these trusted, well-known medical resources state that while the cause of fibromyalgia is unknown, that they also state that there is no cure. I must play devil's advocate and ask: ***"If you don't know what the cause is, how can you know that there is no cure?"***

What you believe about what the medical professionals have to say about there being no cause and no cure for fibromyalgia may be a contributing factor that defines whether or not you are giving yourself the permission and power you have within yourself to send fibro packing.

When you find yourself facing an unexplained chronic condition, rather than blindly believing everything you read or being convinced by unsubstantiated opinions that could change tomorrow, a more valuable and irrefutable approach would be to take this all with a grain of salt, keep an open mind, cultivate a positive attitude and carry out your own research.

2. The Environment

While everyone will be different when it comes to sleuthing out what hidden causes may have contributed to your fibromyalgia diagnosis, besides poor lifestyle choices, there may also be other hidden dangers you may have not previously contemplated that could be at least part of the cause.

a) Noise pollution

Environmental noise pollution (or sound pollution) is another one of those invisible dangers that has the power to wreak havoc with your health. Our world has become increasingly louder, and all this noise is negatively impacting the health of millions of humans (and wildlife) whether or not they are consciously aware of it.

Our once tranquil world now barely has a moment of peace and quiet. The ever-increasing decibel sounds created by humans around the globe means that instead of being able to listen to the rustling of leaves (20 to 30 decibels) we are listening to a constant din of irritating noise caused by trains, planes, automobiles, ambulances and so much more.

The most dangerous thing about noise pollution is that you get used to it, learn to largely ignore it, and become desensitized and unaware of the negative affect it is having on your health.

Some experts say that noise levels below 70 decibels (dB) are *"generally considered to be safe"*, and that anything above 85 dB has the potential to *"damage your hearing over time"*. That doesn't mean that being subjected to constant noise levels above 70 decibels is not affecting your health in other ways.

You may not be aware that besides those loud rock concerts you may have attended, there are many commonly accepted levels of noise in your everyday environment that far exceed *"safe"*. The following is a short list of noises commonly heard, every day in most environments, that exceed what is considered to be the safe 70 dB level:
Doorbell: 80 dB
Ringing Telephone: 80 dB
Coffee Grinder: 80 dB
Air Conditioner: 82 dB
Heavy Traffic: 85 dB
Barking Dog: 90 dB
Earphones listening to music: 100 dB
Blender: 90 dB
Garbage Disposal: 95 dB
Hair Dryer: 95 dB
Lawnmower: 95 dB
Factory Machinery: 100 dB
Snowmobile: 100 dB
Video Arcade: 110 dB

Power Saw: 110 dB
Leaf Blower: 110 dB
Motorcycle: 110 dB
Car Horn: 110 dB
Subway: 115 dB
Ambulance Siren: 120 dB
Rock Concert: 120 dB
Chainsaw: 125 dB
Automobile Stereo: 125 dB
Power Drill: 130 dB
Jet Engine Taking Off: 150 dB
Firecracker: 150 dB

Granted that while some of these noise disturbances may be a fleeting nuisance, they can, over time, have an accumulative effect that can cause more than just damage to your hearing. Over time you get used to all the unnatural noises and because of this may be unaware that there are more worrisome threats to your health and wellbeing to be concerned about with respect to ever-increasing levels of noise pollution. You may be unaware that the World Health Organization considers noise from traffic to be:

"One of the worst environmental stressors for humans."

Further, you cannot expect to receive the quality of sleep you need when nighttime noise levels are above 30 dB. How many of us are lucky enough to live in an environment where the most invasive noise to disturb early morning sleep might be the crowing of a distant rooster or a church bell ringing on a Sunday morning?

Now the world population (including birds and animals) are rarely free from the constant, invasive, disturbingly irritating roar of traffic. In far too many urbanized locations, the never-ending cacophony of sound means that it's almost impossible to get the restful sleep we need to wake up refreshed so that we can face our days with a healthy mind and body.

Constant exposure to noise pollution is known to cause an incredibly long list of health issues, such as:

- Aggression
- Anti-social behaviors
- Decreased attention level
- Decreased mental health
- Diabetes
- Elevated blood pressure

- Headache
- Heart disease
- Hypertension
- Impaired immune system
- Impaired reading skills
- Inflammation
- Irritability
- Memory impairment
- Obesity
- Poor quality sleep
- Premature death
- Stress
- Tinnitus
- [Fibromyalgia]

It is my personal experience that the above list of health issues, said to be caused by noise pollution, is hardly inclusive, because I strongly believe that fibromyalgia should be included in this list. I believe that being subjected to constant noise pollution (even though we may not be consciously aware of it) is like being constantly prodded with a sharp stick. I am not saying that traffic noise causes fibromyalgia but it could well be a contributing factor in the world we live in these days.

Who amongst us would be forever immune to contracting any number of chronic health-related conditions when we are literally living amidst a life of constant interruption?

What can we do to lessen our personal level of noise pollution?

While of course this is a challenging question to answer because your living or working environment might be totally different from my own, there are certainly many common-sense steps you can take. Besides the more obvious, such as not choosing to live beside a freeway, airport, or rail line, there are several steps you could take to help protect yourself from the noise pollution around you:

Free:

- Close windows
- Listen to calming, healing music
- Lower the volume (TV, music, videos)
- Stay away from noisier areas (airports, construction sites)
- Teach your dog not to bark
- Turn off appliances when not in use
- Vote for lowered speed limits in urban areas
- Vote for noise reducing road surfaces

Payable:

- Buy coffee beans that are already ground
- Consider acoustic wall panels
- Create a sound-proof room
- Install a fence (barriers absorb noise)
- Lubricate machinery to reduce noise
- Plant trees (reduces noise by 5 to 10 dB)
- Repair noisy pipes
- Replace older noisy appliances
- Use double-pane windows
- Use earplugs
- Use insulation in walls
- Use wall-to-wall carpeting (hardwood is noisy)
- Wear noise cancelling headphones

While you can no doubt think of other simple noise-reducing solutions or habits, the first step to eliminating the ever-increasing noise pollution we are all subject to these days, is to acknowledge that it is a hidden danger that is harmful to your health.

Now that you are aware of it, you can do something about it. Outside of your own home, perhaps you will want to step-up awareness in your neighborhood. Be proactive to help ensure that city planners are doing all they can to create a healthier living environment with much less noise pollution.

b) EMF pollution

First, a brief explanation about what Electro Magnetic Frequency (EMF) pollution is and how long the human race has been exposed to these fields that were not naturally created. This means human made fields that have been created outside the earth's own natural magnetic field.

In its simplest form, EMF is a combination of electrical and magnetic fields that are produced by moving electrical charges. While your own body creates a natural electrical current, that is required for all bodily functions, what is concerning about artificially created EMFs, is the detrimental affect they may be having on your health.

You may not be aware that up until approximately 100 years ago, your only exposure to electric and magnetic fields was completely natural, and thus could not interfere with or have any detrimental effects on your own energy field. Now, human made EMFs are so prevalent in your daily environment because they are part of the conveniences of our modern lifestyle and are virtually to be found anywhere that we create, generate or use electricity.

This means that it is now almost impossible to totally remove yourself from invasive EMF pollution, and there is an ongoing debate about whether or not this unnatural daily bombardment of EMFs is harmful to your health.

However, any individual must be able to understand that such a drastic environmental change from zero human created EMFs to being immersed in a daily fog of EMFs, caused by constant use of and exposure to electrical devices, must logically have some effect on your body.

While there is a theory that EMF's are "possibly carcinogenic to humans" this theory has been tossed around for more than a century. How can we simply ignore the fact that those living on this earth today are exposed to 100 million times more artificially created EMFs than our grandparents?

It's not a far stretch if you're thinking that the massive amounts of EMFs surrounding us could be the cause of, or at least contribute to, all the many chronic ailments plaguing society today. We are electrical beings that have learned to exist, almost like a worldwide experiment, living under a very high dose of EMFs that nobody is willing to definitively say is or is not harmful to our health.

Consider for a moment that when your natural flow of electricity, that is required for the health of all your bodily functions, is disrupted or interfered with, that you can become chronically ill. One of those mysterious chronic illnesses is called fibromyalgia.

From the first light bulb to electric vehicles, nuclear power plants and everything in between, we have embraced the ever-increasing conveniences of modern life and learned to exist in a world beneath a blanket of unnatural energy sources.

Have you ever stopped to ask, ***"How convenient are all those modern conveniences when they may be harming my own health?"***

Is it any wonder that all life on earth is suffering from more and more health issues, in younger and younger individuals? Even though the effects of overexposure to EMFs would logically vary from person to person, some of the chronic symptoms may include:

- Anxiety

- Burning, prickling and tingling sensations
- Buzzing or static feeling in the brain
- Depression
- Difficulty sleeping
- Dizziness
- Excessive fatigue
- Feeling stressed or "wired"
- Headaches
- Hives or unexplained rashes
- Hormonal imbalances
- Irritability
- Lack of concentration
- Loss of appetite
- Memory loss
- Nausea
- Restlessness
- Ringing in the ears
- Unexplained body pain
- Unusual, unexplained symptoms
- Weakened immune system

There are many small steps you can take to protect yourself from EMF overload:

- Avoid smart (wireless) appliances
- Avoid wearable devices (headsets, monitors, phones, etc.)
- Communicate via text to keep the phone away from your head
- Consider EMF shielding devices (bed canopies, blankets)
- Don't charge your phone next to your bed
- Eliminate your microwave oven
- Get yourself an EMF meter
- If you are particularly sensitive, re-think an electric vehicle
- Place an EMF shielding device on your cell phone, iPad or laptop
- Place your phone on airplane mode when not in use
- Take a day (or more) off from electronics
- Take supplements to protect against exposure (Magnesium, Zinc, Glutathione, Curcumin, Resveratrol, Rosemary extract)
- Turn off the Wi-Fi router (especially at nighttime)
- Use a corded landline (the base produces high levels of radiation)
- Use a corded mouse and keyboard
- Use the speaker function on cell phones
- Use Y-shield paint on your walls (to stop EMF's from entering your living or workspace)

If you are one of those people who simply don't believe that EMFs can be harmful, perhaps you should keep in mind that just because you can't see it, doesn't mean that it can't adversely affect your health.

c) Light pollution

Although light pollution can be seen, it is still worth mentioning here simply because it creates more health-related concerns than you may be currently aware of.

First, what exactly is light pollution (also called photo pollution)? The experts consider light pollution to be the excessive use of artificial light sources during the nighttime. You may not be aware that since the first incandescent light bulb (1879) that there is now so much unnatural light at nighttime that many of us are living under a dome-like shield of light referred to as ***"skyglow"***.

Light pollution has joined the ranks of many other forms of pollution on our Earth because too much light at night can be seriously detrimental to the environment as well as your health. Beyond the more obvious effects of missing out on being able to enjoy the stars and celestial bodies of the night sky, as a result of light pollution, apparently 37% of people living in North America are unable to utilize the full potential of their night vision.

You've all heard about circadian rhythm. For those of you who may need a refresher about how these neurological changes regularly occur over each 24-hour period, the circadian rhythm is your body's clock that regulates your sleep/wake cycle according to light.

When the sun sinks below the horizon and day evolves into the lower light levels of night, your body will naturally release melatonin (a hormone), which in turn induces a feeling of tiredness which regulates your sleep cycles. However, unnatural night-time light pollution can slow or prevent the natural production of melatonin in your body so that your sleep clock is thrown out of balance. It's no wonder that to get those essential 7 to 8 hours of undisturbed sleep, that so many people are adding melatonin supplements to their routine.

It's not only humans that are suffering from light pollution. Satellite images clearly demonstrate that the planet is getting brighter and brighter, and the concern is that this is seriously affecting you, me, animals, birds and the entire ecosystem.

With respect to your compromised health, it's not just the inconvenience of a disturbed sleep clock and waking up feeling tired the next day that is the problem. It is known that night-time light pollution, especially the blue/white LED variety (that is getting worse every year) can have much more serious health concerns, including:

- Cancer
- Depression
- Diabetes
- Heart Disease
- Immune Suppression
- Impaired Daytime Functioning
- Irritability
- Obesity

What can you do to reduce light pollution where you live?
While your individual circumstance will be unique, there are simple steps you can take to reduce this hazard to your health:

Free:

- Avoid the use of blue light at night
- Be aware of using minimal lighting at night
- Become involved in passing dark sky legislation
- Reduce the use of decorative lighting during festive seasons
- Set your computer and phone to "Blue Light Filter"
- Turn off lights when not in use
- Use covered bulbs that face downward

Payable:

- Purchase lights that are DSI (DarkSky International) approved
- Use colored (amber, red, yellow) lights for night lighting
- Use core glow stones and aggregate to light walkways
- Use low-glare outdoor lighting
- Use outdoor motion sensors for security
- Use warm-colored LED lighting

Finally, carry out your own research and learn how light pollution is not only adversely affecting your health and blocking your view of the heavens, but also negatively affecting wildlife, and contributing to climate change while wasting money and energy. Turn off those lights.

3. Toxic Overload

I can hear you saying, *"What on earth is toxic overload?"* This is another one of those hidden dangers that you may have never considered when wondering why fibromyalgia has found its way into your life.

Toxic overload, just as the name implies, is too many toxins. In this case I am referring to an accumulation of harmful toxic substances that have entered your body through inhalation, absorption and ingestion. Toxic substances, because of unwise lifestyle choices (food, water, cleaning products, air pollution, etc.), slowly accumulate in your system over many years and settle into joints, bones and fat tissues that will eventually emerge as health issues.

Think of your body like a large rain barrel that's been catching drips from a leaky gutter system. A few drips may not be anything to worry about at first, but then nobody notices and after a few years the rain barrel has reached full capacity, and that accumulation of tiny drips is now overflowing and running down the outside of the barrel.

When the toxic overload becomes greater than what your body is capable of filtering, this is likely when things begin to go wrong on the health front as you slow down, feel tired more quickly, lose sleep and aches and pains begin to appear for what seems like no apparent reason.

This silent danger has been slowly progressing over time and most likely will eventually appear in the form of many different signs, such as:

- Accelerating aging
- Anxiety
- Bad breath
- Brain fog
- Chronic fatigue
- Constipation
- Dark circles under the eyes
- Depression
- Difficulty concentrating
- Difficulty sleeping
- Digestive problems
- Hair loss
- Headaches or migraines
- Increased risk of cancer
- Increased risk of cardiovascular disease
- Increased risk of Parkinson's
- Joint aches and pains
- Lack of energy
- Memory loss
- Mood swings
- Muscle pains
- Nausea
- Skin conditions
- Sugar cravings
- Weight gain

Many of the symptoms listed above also hold true for anyone suffering from fibro. It is my opinion that toxic overload is a very real hidden danger that, in many cases, may well be a contributing factor to fibromyalgia.

4. The Self-Fulfilling Prophecy

What is a *"self-fulfilling prophecy"?* This is when your expectations about a particular situation (whether warranted or not) causes that situation to come true. Really understanding what the following eight words mean is so far-reaching that it needs to be repeated many times over.

"You are what you believe yourself to be."
~ Paul Coelho ~

When considering the hidden dangers of being diagnosed with fibromyalgia, you absolutely need to add your own expectations and what you believe to be true to this list. OK, let's get clear about how what you may believe could also be a hidden danger to your health. We all grow up with certain beliefs that we often learn from our parents, teachers, co-workers, friends and neighbors. Most of the time these beliefs are designed to help us grow into adulthood and navigate our world as safely as possible.

However, if your own believe system, for whatever reason, may also include blindly believing everything you are told, without question, especially when considering your own health, this can result in giving away your own power, which can be an impediment to healing yourself.

I am not trying to say that you should never believe what your medical professional tells you, but rather that you should always question any diagnosis and always carry out your own research if you were diagnosed with fibromyalgia.

With respect to being diagnosed with fibromyalgia, going beyond the boundaries of the traditional medical system and carrying out your own research is especially important because to simply accept what you are being told sets that old, self-fulfilling prophecy in motion. Consider that there have been many very strong medical opinions drawn over the years that during their time were rarely questioned, and were blindly believed to be true, until they weren't.

Relying upon the opinions of those who admit that they don't know the cause, and yet looking no farther than your own learned belief system, or what you are told by others, that may not have been updated for many years, could be the very reason why you are having difficulties winning the fibro battle.

It is my sincere hope that since you are reading this book, that you have already broken free from the shackles of the self-fulfilling prophecy, and that you will see the wisdom in questioning everything.

Living your best life means looking beyond the parameters of the medical opinion because you believe that being in charge of your own health is one of the most important tasks you will ever undertake.

"Self-care is the greatest middle finger of all time."
~ Unknown ~

Believing that you have within you the power to heal yourself is the first step toward giving fibro the finger.

"Wake up – Kick Ass – Repeat"

Chapter 5: You ARE Powerful!

A diagnosis of fibromyalgia can often create great feelings of depression and despair, especially if you believe all that you are being told by the mainstream medical community. To treat yourself, you need to strongly embrace your own power.

I will begin this chapter with a quote from a very famous children's book author (Dr. Seuss), who said:

***"You have brains in your head. You have feet in your shoes.
You can steer yourself any direction you choose.
You're on your own. And you know what you know.
And YOU are the one who'll decide where to go."***

You may not be aware that once you accept something, you give it great power over you. This is true for both positive and negative things you may have accepted into your life. With respect to fibromyalgia, it's possible that you may be finding yourself here at this moment in life because of your life path up until now.

You may never have imagined that being burdened with this painful and apparently unexplained malady at this point in your life is something you yourself may have had an unconscious hand in creating.

1. You Are the Master

To cure yourself of any sort of malady, you need to first accept that **you are the master of your own destiny.**

Once you accept that it is entirely possible that the choices you have made in this current lifetime have brought you here, you then have the power to release yourself from anything that may have been getting in the way of creating a positive future for the improved, new you.

When I look back on my own life, I am often reminded that things happened that appeared to be negative at the time and not consciously something I wanted. However, it was something I needed to help me make different life choices that would better support my future mental and physical wellbeing so I could move toward the next, better phase of my life.

Consider that some of us need stronger *"messages"* that can be either verbal or physical before we take a step back and realize that moving forward requires change.

Pain is a very strong motivator and throughout my journey with fibro, I have learned to accept that I needed this painful wake-up call to steer me in a different and much happier and healthier direction.

Please hear me when I say:

"You can't recover until you know what you're recovering from."

A great part of my own personal experience with fibromyalgia has been the discovery of what I was recovering from because this goes much deeper than the actual physical pain you may be feeling. Once you discover this, you will be well on your way to a better you.

2. Super Syndrome

My first inkling that major change was required on my part was when I finally accepted that maintaining a lifetime of being superwoman had, over many years, resulted in creating a very damaging relationship with myself. While being superwoman (or superman) may not be something you need to concern yourself with, note that there is a *"superwoman syndrome"*.

This *"super"* syndrome woman is in pursuit of perfection in all areas of her life. Wow! That described me to a T, and while this is not the place to get into what life experiences led me to become a superwoman, because that would be another entire book, I've said before that this type of lifestyle or A-personality type is often associated with fibromyalgia. During my earlier years, I had no idea that my superwoman lifestyle choices were not doing me any great favors. They were leaving me open to needing to hear, or in this case feel, a very big and painful message that reared its ugly head in the form of fibromyalgia.

It's common knowledge that women are known to be more efficient at multi-tasking, which leaves them more easily open to taking on too much all at once. However, it doesn't matter what gender you identify with: too much is just too much.

"Never get so busy making a living that you forget to make a life."
~ Dolly Parton ~

If you've been pushing yourself too hard to succeed, and are feeling overworked, stressed and having difficulties coping with the day-to-day seemingly endless aspects of your life, it's time to take a serious look at what needs to be changed.

You cannot be the best for yourself, your family or anyone else around you when you don't give yourself time to pause and take care of your own personal needs. This means being aware of the small (or large) signs and messages, such as chronic fatigue, headaches, depression, feeling stressed and overwhelmed, and having difficulty sleeping that may soon lead to the unexplained chronic pain known as fibromyalgia.

No matter who you are, and what lifestyle choices may have brought you here now, I know all too well from personal experience that a relentless pursuit of perfection will eventually create adverse, and in the case of fibro, very painful consequences in your life.

Again, I will say to you, ***"You can't recover until you know what you are recovering from"*** so rather than simply ignoring what lifestyle choices may have contributed to a painful life lesson, scroll back the time and take an honest look at yourself. Once acceptance of your past is part of your new life, you will have given yourself the power to do the work involved in building an exciting new path toward the life you really want.

Write down below what in your past may have brought you to what I call the *"fibro wake-up call"*.

3. The Power of Acceptance

Having the ability to accept all aspects of your life (both good and bad) is not weak or an admission of failure, just the opposite. Accepting every aspect of yourself and the circumstances in which you currently find yourself will give you the motivation and power you need to turn them in a positive direction. Carl Jung, famous founder of analytical psychology, is often quoted as having coined the following thought-provoking words:

"What you resist, persists."
~ Carl Jung ~

Really take a good look at those 4 words and grasp what they mean: the more you resist anything in life, the more you bring it to you. Life isn't about what happens to you but how you respond to it. When you find yourself fighting against your current reality – in this case fibromyalgia - you are placing a roadblock in the way of taking your first step toward transforming this chronic condition and removing it from your life. The power of acceptance is simply telling yourself the truth about your situation. Take the time to write down below everything that is causing you pain, anxiety, stress, etc. Once you have your list in front of you, the way forward is to be honestly willing to simply accept them as they are today.

Look at what you have written, and then give yourself permission to say, *"Yes, I recognize and accept that everything on this list is my current reality."*

Once you can do this, and have fully accepted that yes, fibro is currently part of your life, you will gain a sense of peace and a feeling of power that is the beginning of the end of your suffering. With the power of acceptance also comes a clarity and purpose of mind about moving forward with the focused goal of making fibro a distant past memory.

4. The Power of Positive Thinking

Yes, you've heard this all before, but have you really given yourself the opportunity to really understand the amazing truth behind the power of positive thinking?

"Sometimes when things are falling apart, they may actually be falling into place."
~ J. Lynn ~

Do we truly live up to the potential of those big brains that we all carry about? We've all heard the myth that, on average, we use approximately 10% of our brains. However, it has been proven that you use every part of your 3-pound (1.36 kg) brain, and much closer to the truth of that 10% myth is that you may only *"understand"* about 10% of how that complex organ functions.

Rather than worrying about how your amazingly powerful and complex brain functions, when using it to combat pain of unknown origin, all you need to do is simply accept the fact that your brain is a powerful tool that can help you to overcome almost any obstacle life may throw in your path. You may not be aware that pain, or the sensation of pain, begins in the brain. This is where the power of positive thinking can come to your rescue and really help to win the war against the fickle fibromyalgia.

Your brain is so powerful, that once stressors have been identified, it will signal to the rest of your body a flight or fight (run or stay from a stressful situation) response, and in turn, this creates very real physical effects that can be felt as pain. Chronic pain is nothing more than the brain signalling to the central nervous system that it should continue to put these learned pain patterns at the forefront of your daily life. In other words, fibromyalgia is nothing more than a learned chronic cycle of pain and stress that continues to repeat itself.

Now, take a moment to think about this and let it really settle into your mind. If the brain is powerful enough to create a chronic cycle of pain, should you just accept this, or instead realize that you can choose to create a different outcome? Of course, the correct answer is that once you **accept that your brain is powerful enough to plunge you into a cycle of chronic pain, it is also powerful enough to break this debilitating cycle.**

This is where becoming aware of how your thoughts are keeping your brain on the same learned path of daily pain comes into play. When your day is consumed by negative feelings, thoughts and written or spoken words, there is no room for change or for something better to emerge. The more you think: *"I have so much pain"* or *"It hurts all the time",* the more pain messages your body receives. Thinking negative thoughts means telling your brain how terrible everything is and your brain will tell your body!

On the one hand, the brain can learn to make the body feel pain, while on the other hand, the brain can just as easily unlearn the pattern of sending pain signals to the body.

Never forget the connection between your brain and your pain!

a) You are what you think you are

No truer words have been spoken, than the 7 written below, when it comes down to sending messages to your powerful brain.

"You are what you think you are."

~ Confusius ~

Whether you are currently aware of it, or not, your daily thoughts have a profound impact on your mood, your feelings of worth and self-confidence, and the choices you make, all of which can be reflected in your health.

First, you need to acknowledge that your day may be filled with negative words and thoughts that you may not have been previously aware of. You may have been unknowingly helping to solidify your brain's learned pain patterns and unconsciously telling your brain that chronic pain is now what you can expect for the rest of your life.

If this is something you've been doing, now is the time to change that pattern and the easiest and quickest way to begin this change is to write all your negative words, thoughts or phrases down on paper.

You may be thinking: *"I feel terrible" – "My back hurts" - "I'm so tired all the time" – "Everything is painful" – "My life sucks".*

Write down all your negative words and thoughts on the **left** side of the writing area. I will explain what to write on the right side soon.

Now, take a good look at what you've written because this is what you think you are. Rather than believing all those negative words and phrases, it's time to tell your brain a different, more positive story, instead.

Always remember that: ***You are what you think you are.***

OK, now you're learning how powerful your thoughts and beliefs can be, so how can you change all those painful, negative thoughts and feelings you've been having into ones that have the power to alleviate the unexplained fibro pains that are keeping you from your best life?

Take another close look at those negative words you've been giving all your power to and instead find ways to turn the negative into a positive.

Perhaps you wrote down *"My life sucks"* and you're wondering how to turn that phrase into something positive. I'm certain that when you really think about what those words mean, you will realize this is most likely an exaggeration and that you have much to celebrate in your life.

Therefore, rather than continuing to tell your powerful brain to keep you on the same path of feeling stress and chronic pain, change your pain story and instead replace *"My life sucks"* with a different phrase that will take you down a new path and make you feel much happier and grateful for all that is good in your life. Forget about constantly training your brain to believe that your life sucks, and instead say something like: *"I'm so happy to be alive because I'm learning how to end my pain cycle and live my happy, best life."*

Once you realize how you are hurting yourself by allowing negative thoughts to speak to you, and how easy it can be to tell your powerful brain to replace negative thoughts with positive ones, you will quickly begin to see positive results.

Go back to your negative word list and rewrite them. Turn each word or phrase into something positive and write it on the right side.

Here's a few examples:

"I'm so tired" becomes *"Soon I will have the energy I need."*
"I feel terrible" becomes *"I'm learning about how I can feel better."*
"My back hurts" becomes *"A swim will make me feel better."*

You get the idea – now go and turn all your negatives into positives and feel so much better with the power of positive thinking.

Here are few inspiring quotes that you may find helpful:

"Your mind influences your happiness and health."
~ Victoria B. Allen ~

"What you think, you will become."
~ Buddha ~

"Once you take all the negatives in your life and turn them into positives, more positives will quickly follow."
~ Victoria B. Allen ~

"One small positive thought in the morning can change your whole day."
~ Zig Ziglar ~

"A positive attitude gives you power over your circumstances instead of your circumstances having power over you."
~ Joyce Meyer ~

"A positive attitude may not solve all your problems, but it will annoy enough people to make it worth the effort."
~ Herm Albright ~

b) Set your intention

Once you realize that harnessing the power of your own amazing mind can bring about the positive changes you need and want in your life, and you're on the path to turning any negative thoughts into positive ones, all you need now is to set your intention.

What does it mean to *"Set your intention"?* Simply, all this means is to direct your consciousness (by saying out loud or to yourself) to check in with yourself and be aware of what you want to create as an experience in your life each day.

Setting your intention as you greet each day, rather than just allowing the day to randomly unfold, truly has the power to change your life.

When you approach your day with the right mindset and acknowledge your own reminders to stay committed to the steps it will take to get there, you will be much more likely to avoid any distractions that may steer you off your intended course and distract you from your goals.

Here's a simple routine for setting your daily intention:
Before you roll out of bed in the morning, pause and check in with yourself by asking yourself what you want to accomplish today. Then focus for a moment on your *"to do"* list for this day. Think about what

sort of energy you want to apply to the things you want to accomplish today.

Lastly, get out your journal and write down your daily intentions. They can be the same for each day, or entirely different each day. You might write:

- Accomplish one thing on my to do list
- Acknowledge all that is good in my life
- Focus on my to do list (write the list)
- Have less pain in my life each day
- Smile more, laugh more
- Take a 15-minute break to meditate
- Take notice of what my intuition is telling me
- Turn any negative thoughts into positive ones

What should be on your intention list?
There is no definitive answer to that question because everyone is unique, and we all have vastly different goals for ourselves. If you are suffering from the slings and arrows that fibromyalgia can bring into your life, it's very likely that one of the most important things that will stand out for you will be recovery from fibro.

Of course, there will be other goals or accomplishments that may be foremost in your life, so no matter what they may be, don't forget to add these to your intention list, too.

Lastly, when creating your intention list, keep in mind that (a) this is not an exercise in perfection; (b) there are no wrong answers; and (c) your list will take on a life of its own with many changes over time.

"Always believe that you have the power to create something wonderful - Right Now."
~ Victoria B. Allen ~

Here's some blank space for you to write what feels relevant for your daily intention list, so you can start living your intentional life right now:

"Wake up – Kick Ass – Repeat"

Chapter 6: Motivational Swear Words

When you are suffering from the daily pain of fibromyalgia, any little thing that grants you a moment of relief, including trotting out some choice swear words, is always welcome. Let's not kid ourselves – everybody swears, even parrots. Even those who have taken a vow of silence will swear on the inside when they just stubbed their toe. Swearing can be a good way to let go of the frustration you feel.

***"There ought to be a room in every house to swear in.
It's dangerous to have to repress an emotion."***
~ Mark Twain ~

However, should you happen to be one of those rare individuals that never has experienced the use of the 4-letter-words, please don't be offended by this chapter, as this is certainly not my intention.

I'm not trying to change your ways and turn you into a swearing machine. I'm simply suggesting that if you do swear, that you realize how swear words can be motivational as well as pain relieving.

Studies have proven that when you swear during a physically painful episode, doing so can help you to tolerate the pain, and that swearing can help to release feelings of frustration, which then leads to a calming effect.

When used responsibly, swearing can be especially effective when you are dealing with a painful, chronic condition and everything is feeling out of your control.

What are your favorite swear words (for instance when your fibro pain is driving you mad)? Write them down below and really enjoy using them with energy and conviction.

I'll help you get started by sharing my favorite *"swear phrase"* that is so stupid that it makes me smile every time. This is only an exercise for you, so please feel free to fill in the blanks (or not,) or make up your own.

"Sh*t, F*ck, Bloody Hell, Life Sucks"

Then I learned a simple change or tag that I added to my favorite swear phrase, that made a big difference in how much power I was giving to my pain… ***"But I'm still standing!"***

Yes, swear words can be motivational and a tremendous tool for coping with pain management and the stronger the swear word (you know which ones those are), the more positive the pain-relieving effect (that is, unless you already regularly swear like a rum-soaked pirate on vacation).

Besides helping to reduce pain, swearing helps you to realize that you have more power than you might be currently feeling. Here's a few more examples you might enjoy:

- Daily life is 10% what happens to you and 90% how many times you say "SH*T" throughout the day.

- Life begins at the end of my comfort zone and there's nothing F*ing comfortable about fibro.

- When life conjures up tough situations, I don't waste time feeling sorry for myself, I say: *"Bring it on!"*

- I do whatever it is that I must do, until I can do whatever I F*ing want to do.

- There is nothing that I cannot do, and I F*ing **will**.

- It doesn't matter how slowly I move, as long as I keep F*ing moving!

I'm sure you can think of many more swear words and phrases that will personally resonate with you, so the next blank page is your chance to write some of them down, so you can feel better right now. [F*** this sh*t!] [Cheer the F*** Up!]. Perhaps write them on a separate page (not in this book) if you don't want other people to know your swear words. 😊

"Wake up – Kick Ass – Repeat"

Chapter 7: The Life Race and Your Mind

Moving through your life too quickly or piling too much on your plate can certainly put you at higher risk for fibromyalgia.

Is your life a race and are you racing through your life like the blurring speed of a hummingbird?? Are you always seeking out better, faster, or more efficient ways to get through your days? Today we all live in a society of instant gratification: a quick-fix, quick-must-have culture. You are never out of touch because you go everywhere with a smart phone that can give you everything you need at a moment's notice.

"Instant gratification takes too long."
~ Carrie Fisher ~

Consequently, you don't have to carry a calendar, compass, calculator, camera, flashlight, measuring tape, pen, note pad, book. You don't have to go to a grocery store or any other shop to buy what you need, stop at the bank to pay your bills or wait until you get home to call your friends.

You no longer go to the library to carry out research, wait until you get home to read a newspaper, check the stock market, or watch videos, the local news, or your favorite TV show because you have it all in the palm of your hand, ready to access immediately. While technology has certainly made lives more efficient, over the years, life has become more and more of a swift moving blur as we all race through our days at top speed.

If your life is a race, what are you racing toward? Don't you have time to slow down a little bit and stop getting caught up in a life of instant gratification? Do you want to get to the end of life faster or with more peace, happiness and appreciation of each day?

We are constantly bombarded by endless noise that irritates, interactive devices that distract and shortened time frames for almost everything. We've become like a short-circuiting electrical device ourselves, receiving information in bits and pieces that last only brief moments. We are not able to slow our minds and really concentrate on anything for more than a few seconds.

A big problem in society these days that your mind never stops. You wake up with the noise of an alarm, you check your messages, get the kids up, get them ready for school, start your workday, sit on computer for hours, get lunch, back to the computer, travel home for food, do washing, get kids bathed and put them to bed, check your to do list for the next day. Watch some movies on streaming platforms, browse through channels for 1 hour to decide what to watch. From the first step out of bed until the last step into your bed at night you read your phone messages.

Your daily schedule might be different, but you know where I am going with this: your mind never stops! I don't know about you, but I understand why in "the olden days" people were generally healthier and nobody ever heard about fibromyalgia. The main reason, I think, is because people used to go to work (not on a computer) and move all day long. Go home after work, sit down without distractions to have a meal and then: relax e.g. do some knitting, read books, read the newspaper. No TV, no movie channels. Their busy minds turn into calm minds before going to bed.

Excessive living

We've all heard about excessive eating but what about excessive living?

Scrolling, drinking, eating, sitting, more scrolling, more eating, watching Netflix ©, scrolling, watching more Netflix © and more scrolling. These are all actions that give us temporary "satisfaction" or "pleasure". It is living in a state of excessive consumption. It is sensory overload. It has become an addiction for many people: addiction to temporary pleasure.

Our brain and nervous system are constantly bombarded with far too much information than we can healthily cope with so our brain becomes overwhelmed and cannot process all the data.

We are not supposed to be exposed to this constant bombardment of stimulation and our mind gives us signs to warn us: we can't focus, we become irritable, we can't sleep, we become anxious, we have a feeling of too much stress. We need to do things in moderation, not in excess.

I've already mentioned the mind-body connection and I hope you understand the importance of calming your mind now and again. Your mind needs a break too, just like your body does.

Your mind never stops! Do something about it!

Guess what? You've been dying since the day you were born, so why not learn how to slow down and enjoy every little moment because the truth is that none of us are going to be here forever. We shall all arrive at the end of this lifetime soon enough. In the meantime, do yourself a favour and find out how to live your best life, just the way you want it to be **right now**, because there is no race.

When you finally realize that pretty much everything you were taught to believe that was important to achieve on that racing hamster wheel of life actually isn't, and instead learn how to slow your roll, find real life in every moment and joy in all the little things, you have already won.

Your mind made you ill, not your anatomy of your body.

"Wake up – Kick Ass – Repeat"

Chapter 8: Fibro Recovery on a Small Budget

When looking for a cure for any sort of medical condition, all too often how much help you receive and how quickly you can begin feeling better is directly related to how much money you can afford to spend.

The budget-minded need not despair, because relief can still be found for zero cost or by raiding your piggy bank.

While it's true that not everyone may be able to afford the many treatments available when battling the slings and arrows of fibro, it's also true that there is much improvement and even total elimination to be had for the budget-minded, self-help individual seeking to rid themselves of fibro pain.

The chapter (Pills, Potions & Paraphernalia) outlines many helpful modalities and their respective costs. This chapter is devoted to the many low or zero cost things you can do to help rid yourself of the daily challenges that fibro can bring to your life.

In other words, while curing yourself of fibro should never require a second mortgage on your home, it is very important to make that connection between mind and body because healing can begin for zero cost when you have a calm, peaceful mind.

1. Attitude Adjustment

Often the most powerful way we can help ourselves to feel better, both physically and mentally requires a simple *"attitude adjustment."*

"You can often change your circumstances by changing your attitude."
~ Eleanor Roosevelt ~

OK, I hear you asking, *"What's wrong with my attitude and what's adjusting it, or changing it got to do with feeling better?"*

You may not be consciously aware of how the many variables (education, family, friends, colleagues, etc.) you encounter throughout your lifetime may adversely affect your own attitude and how you react to what you are dealing with in the moment.

The following sections are designed to remind you about how a little attitude tune-up can really be beneficial, not just when giving fibromyalgia its early walking papers, but also to help make all aspects of your life a much more enjoyable journey.

a) Retrain your all-powerful brain

Re-read the chapter "You ARE Powerful", because a very large part of breaking free from the pain of **fibromyalgia is the belief that you really do have the power to heal yourself.**

Of course, those automatic, unconscious thought patterns can be challenging to re-train. However, it's only the negative unconscious thought patterns that you need to be aware of re-training.

You've heard the saying before that ***"practice makes perfect"*** and while you may have thought this was only relevant when learning how to excel at some sort of physical activity, practicing is also very important when re-training your brain.

Just the same as becoming the best at any sort of physical activity requires focus, the same is true for re-training your brain to believe that yes, you do have the ability to heal yourself.

The following exercises may help you to cut through distracting self-chatter so that you can regain and strengthen your own power to succeed.

Meditate: this is a simple and free way to begin the re-training of your brain (I will discuss more later) because even brief, daily meditation helps to activate new neural brain pathways that will help you to slow down and learn to focus on just one thing.

Just one thing: In today's fast-paced world of instant gratification there are few that haven't been caught up in a storm of multi-tasking.

While it used to be thought that the ability to multi-task was an efficient way to get through your days, the reality is that much of society has lost the ability to engage at a deeper level of focus on one task.

Instead, all that switching from task to task is just skimming the surface of each task and leaving you with many things unfinished and feeling mentally exhausted.

To achieve a higher level of success and regain all that power your brain is capable of means learning how to re-train your focus so that you can do just one thing at a time, do it well and finish it.

Self-awareness: again, re-read the chapter "You ARE Powerful" because being self-aware is a powerful tool that helps you to recognize when you may have slipped back into a negative thought pattern.

It's important to practice checking in with yourself so that you learn to identify (and re-write) those negative thoughts that can prevent you from achieving your goals.

If you're feeling that your forward momentum is on hold, it could be something as simple as an unconsciously negative thought whispering in your ear telling you that *"This is too much work"*, or *"I can't do this."* Rather than giving up, realize that negative thoughts are simply your brain sending you feedback, and all this feedback is an opportunity to be self-aware and practice your re-writing skills.

The truth is that once you focus on putting the power of your mind to work, you can achieve anything.

b) Accept what is now
You've found yourself in this situation for any number of reasons that likely began long ago when you consciously or unconsciously made various life choices and accepted certain belief systems. This quote bears reminding once again:

"You can't recover until you know precisely what it is that you're recovering from."

All this means is that you need to recognize what may have contributed to you being burdened with fibro and simply accept what is happening in your life right now. Acceptance gives you the power to devise a plan to change what is no longer serving you. Once you accept that fibro is a part of your life right now, you can begin to forge a new path forward and re-write your future.

c) Be grateful
Expressing gratitude improves your health! Many studies have proven that the simple act of giving thanks for all that you have in your life, even if it doesn't feel exactly the way you want it to be at the moment, can have many positive effects on your health.

"When I started counting my blessings, my whole life turned around."
~Willie Nelson ~

Besides generally improving your outlook on life and feeling more optimistic, acknowledging what you feel grateful for can improve both your mental and physical health. Studies have shown that many areas of your life can benefit from expressing gratitude:

- Better mood
- Decreased anxiety
- Decreased chronic pain
- Decreased depression
- Fewer headaches
- Improved heart health
- Improved sleep
- Stronger immune system

However, just like anything else that is important in your life, learning how to express your gratitude, especially when you may not be feeling your best, takes practice. Perhaps you witnessed a beautiful rainbow, or a kind person made space for you to change lanes when you were driving home, or a friend sent you a funny text.

When you begin to write down these seemingly insignificant little occurrences and take the time to say thank you to those who made your day a little brighter, you will soon discover that there is plenty to be grateful for every day.

Write down the things you are grateful for:

____

____

____

____

____

____

____

____

____

OK, you have written some things down but why not get a diary and start a gratitude journal? It is an easy way to practice feeling grateful for all the little things that were wonderful in your day. Journal about these things by taking a few moments to reflect on your day before bedtime.

d) Color your world

Coloring books are no longer just for kids. Adult coloring books are now widely available and very popular. We are living amidst a highly stress-inducing culture, and as such it's important to find simple ways to unwind and de-stress without choosing to do something that can create even more stress.

The simple, non-competitive, no judgment act of coloring shuts off exterior noise and distractions, and the day's mind chatter, and gives you the gift of being mindful and focusing on just one thing in the present moment.

There are many health benefits attributed to coloring, because removing attention from yourself:

- Calms the nervous system
- Improves brain function
- Improves focus
- Improves mood
- Improves motor skills
- Improves sleep
- Loosens tight muscles
- Reduces anxiety
- Reduces pain
- Relieves stress
- Slows heart rate

Once you begin coloring, you may find that getting out that coloring book becomes your new little *"go to"* indulgence whenever you need a moment of calm in your hectic day.

While any sort of coloring book will be greatly helpful, if you search online with the words *"Fibromyalgia Coloring Book"* you will find many choices for coloring books designed to help relieve chronic pain.

You can even find adult motivational swear word coloring books. You've already learned about how swear words can really help relieve chronic pain, so if you can find a coloring book for motivational swear words, I say, why not?

No matter how much pain I was in when I was working through my fibromyalgia, sitting and coloring for an hour took me totally away from my worries. I felt happy, creative and felt less pain while I was coloring.

A bonus for me was and is, that coloring really improves my sleep quality. Just 30 to 60 minutes of coloring before bed helped to ensure that I enjoyed at least 3 more hours of uninterrupted sleep. That's a big deal when your day is painful and restful sleep is difficult to come by.

Today, I still color every day and feel so much better for it. I would highly recommend that you get yourself some adult coloring books and a set of coloring pencils (low-cost products) and start enjoying this simple, yet highly effective, health-promoting pastime, too.

2. Immerse Yourself in Nature

Imagine a quiet space away from the noise of the city where you can listen to birds and bees, hear leaves fluttering in the treetops, watch waves ebbing and flowing at the seashore, and observe clouds drifting by and changing shape overhead. Don't you feel happier and more relaxed already?

There is so much in nature that can be instrumental in helping to reduce pain and make you feel healthier, and all you need to do is take the time to seek it out.

"In every walk with nature one receives far more than he seeks."
~ John Muir ~

a) Earthing

Earthing (also known as *"grounding"*) means walking barefoot or swimming in a lake or ocean so that the electrical frequency of your energy is physically in touch with the frequency of the Earth's energy.

Clint Ober from Groundology said: "*Many health problems, particularly* ***fibromyalgia****, would appear because we are disconnected from the Earth. The Earth has a strong electromagnetic field, which is well known to sailors: it is what makes the compass needle indicate to the North. In fact, the Earth is like a big electric battery and this battery not only affects compasses and animals but humans too. You are like a phone that re-charges: you must be connected to your electrical network to re-charge your phone. That is pretty much the same for humans but humans need to connect to Earth to recharge."*

When you wade or swim in water or walk barefoot on the grass, walk on a bare patch of earth or across a sandy beach for approximately 30 minutes, unhealthy electrical charges will be dissipated, and you will be reconnected with the natural frequency of the Earth.

While studying earthing is still an under-researched topic, science is beginning to realize that there is significant evidence to support that earthing can be beneficial for healing many common health issues plaguing our society today:

- Anxiety
- Cardiovascular disease
- Chronic pain
- Depression
- Inflammation
- Mood changes
- Muscle damage
- Sleep disorders

My favorite place to practice earthing is at the beach because, as well as being grounded, salt ocean water contains many beneficial minerals that are known to be very healing. Besides breathing in the health-promoting negative ions (increase the flow of oxygen to the brain) that are present in the beach environment, walking barefoot will literally help you to get back into sync with the healing energy of Mother Earth.

b) Visit the seashore

Have you ever wondered why going for a walk in the woods or sitting beside the ocean (or other bodies of moving water) makes you feel more relaxed?

Here's a little bit of science for you – crashing waves produce *"Negative Ions"* which are good for our health. I know it sounds backwards that *"negative"* is good for us, and *"positive"* is bad. This is true when talking about inhaling odourless, invisible oxygen molecules known as negative ions, which are created naturally by the Earth's own radiation field, in combination with air, sunlight and water.

The reason why you feel happier and more alive when around higher concentrations of negative ions is because the negative ions help to purify the air and cause an elevated release of serotonin (a natural mood modulating chemical that your nerve cells produce). Among other things, serotonin helps to alleviate feelings of stress and depression and bring a smile to your face.

Walking along a beach or spending time near a waterfall or deep in a mountain forest, means that you have immersed yourself in nature and removed yourself from noise pollution as well as many of the daily positively charged electrons found in the dust, exhaust, smoke, mold spores and viruses that are prevalent in the city environment.

Negative ions neutralize free radicals (unstable atoms that can damage cells causing aging and illness). Breathing in the natural smells of the woods or beach helps to improve the function of your respiratory tract by diminishing respiratory type illnesses (hay fever, asthma, colds, flu), revitalizing cell metabolism, and increasing the flow of oxygen to the brain to decrease mental fog and help you to feel more mentally alert.

If it's at all possible for you, take the time to go walk on the beach, sit beside a waterfall, or hike through a forest and breathe in those good negative ions because this is a cost-free way to experience a happier and healthier you.

c) Walk in the woods

Of course, there are benefits to attending your local gym so that you can walk your miles on a treadmill. However, much better for your peace of mind and overall health, would be to get away from the noise and air pollution of the city and head to the great outdoors where you can enjoy gentle exercise in tandem with nature.

"The creation of a thousand forests is in one acorn."
~ Ralph Waldo Emerson ~

If you have always thought that prolonged vigorous physical activity is the only way to improve your health, perhaps you need to learn about all the free health benefits that simply strolling through the woods can provide.

Low impact walking for only 30 minutes a day is proven to be a beneficial and simple way to maintain your overall health. Don't believe me? Check out the impressive list of health benefits attributed to a simple 30-minute walk:

- Improved cardiovascular fitness
- Improved muscle power
- Improved pulmonary (lung) fitness
- Increased endurance
- Less joint stiffness
- Less muscle pains
- Reduced body fat
- Reduced risk of cancer
- Reduced risk of heart disease
- Reduced risk of osteoporosis
- Reduced risk of stroke
- Reduced risk of Type 2 diabetes
- Stronger bones

You know what they say – ***"Use it or lose it."*** When you're in pain, it's difficult to even contemplate the simplest of exercise routines, so why not be more realistic and add a simple, low impact, daily stroll to your routine.

Walking is free, and it requires minimal effort for maximum benefit. Also, combining your daily walk with choosing to walk in a nature-inspired environment (in the woods, at a park, by the seashore) will provide you with even more health benefits.

3. The Power of Music

"Where words fail, music speaks."
~ Hans Christian Anderson ~

I was never the type of person who listened to healing music, but it has helped me tremendously in my fibro fight. It is truly unbelievable what good vibes music has given me!

a) Solfeggio frequency
We've all heard that music heals the soul, but what if it can do so much more? "*What is healing music*", you may be asking.

Improving your physical health by harnessing the free healing power of music is not anything new. Most people know that listening to relaxing music is just that – relaxing.

However, what you may not be aware of is that listening to specific music, tones, instruments and sonic vibrations has the power to balance energy and heal both body and mind.

Playing relaxing music has the power to reduce stress, ease feelings of anxiety, lower blood pressure, decrease elevated heart rates, diminish the production of cortisol (some call it the stress hormone) and repair your body.

When you understand that music is vibration, then it makes perfect sense that surrounding yourself with good vibrations will make you feel better on many different levels.

As you will read in further in this book (when I talk about Scalar Wave Therapy), every cell in your body vibrates to an electrical charge that is measured in millivolts (mV) with the optimal charge for a healthy person being between 70 and 90mV.

It's worth really taking note that when the natural electrical charge within your cells begins to diminish due to advancing age or any number of health-related issues, and the charge becomes much less than optimal (below 20 mV) this is when disease begins to set in. Listening to the right frequency of music can help to charge up cells that are not vibrating at the optimal level so that your body can heal itself.

It can be challenging to convince those people that need cold, hard facts and irrefutable scientific proof that what you cannot see, or touch can truly be such an effective free tool when it comes to healing yourself.

However, healing with sound is not a new idea because sound therapy was first utilized by Australian aborigines some 40,000 years ago with the traditional wind instrument known as the didgeridoo.

While by comparison, North American cultures have been slow to catch on to the power of healing music, researchers have now coined the term *"Vibroacoustic Therapy" (VAT),* which Sound Oasis® describes as: *"...the use of low frequency vibrations to stimulate body cells into therapeutic states of relaxation and healing..."*

Although still being careful not to be definitive, the medical field is beginning to suggest that something as simple as a two-pronged tuning fork that vibrates at a specific pitch to penetrate the body at the cellular level may be effective when recovering from injury and relieving chronic bone and muscle pain.

From ancient Egypt where many believe that entire pyramids were designed for the purpose of curing illness through harmonic healing to Tibetan monks. The monks used sound vibrations from singing bowls to lower blood pressure, improve circulation, strengthen the immune system and alleviate pain. This was 6,000 years ago. It is very difficult to ignore that the right sound frequencies can benefit your health.

What are the right sound frequencies and what is some of the science behind them?

The quick answer to that question is any sound frequency that stimulates the cells to produce nitric oxide. As you might imagine, when you age, or your body is fighting disease and inflammation, your body naturally produces less nitric oxide.

Nitric Oxide (NO) is a signalling element or *"messenger molecule"* that transmits signals to cells in the immune, nervous and cardiovascular systems within your body.

When enough nitric oxide is present, cell communication is more efficient, and when the cells are working at optimum level, they can then have the power to heal what ails you.

The more complicated answer is that while there are many different sound frequencies that are beneficial for healing both the mind and the body, the optimum sound frequency for pain and stress relief is believed to be **174Hz,** which is the first and lowest tone in the Solfeggio frequency musical scale.

What is the Solfeggio frequency musical scale and how can it help you on your journey to a happier and healthier you?

The Solfeggio scale was created during the 11th century by Guido d'Arezzo (a Benedictine monk) to teach simple melodies to singers during a time when there was only a small amount of music that had been notated and few who knew how to read it.

The ancient Solfeggio scale was lost some time during the 16th century and replaced by what is known as the *"Twelve Tone Equal Temperament"* that remains in use today.

However, during the 1970's the original Solfeggio scale was re-introduced by Dr. Joseph Puleo (a naturopathic physician) who realized that this scale had the ability to transform wellbeing on a physical, emotional and spiritual level.

Solfeggio frequencies are specific, fundamental tones of sound dating back to ancient spiritual traditions in both Western and Eastern religions that are believed to positively affect both the conscious and unconscious mind to help stimulate healing in the body right down to the DNA level.

Everything in you and around you has a frequency, whether it's a living entity such as a person, animal or plant, or whether it's sound, light, or your individual feelings and thoughts. How you act and feel is your state of being, and this is determined by how high or low your individual frequency may be.

As you might imagine, the higher your personal frequency, the easier and more quickly you can heal, feel happier and find the path of your greatest potential. Following is an outline of some of the most well-known healing frequencies, all of which you can easily find for free on YouTube ©, Spotify © or other online apps. These are identified by the health benefits associated with each one:

174 Hz: "*Pain relief*" frequency

- encourages a sense of safety and love

- enhances courage and inner body energy
- improved concentration
- natural anesthetic
- reduces emotional pain
- reduces pain after surgery for quicker recovery
- relieves lower back, knee, foot and leg pain
- relieves migraine pain
- stress and pain relief

285 Hz: "*Rejuvenation*" frequency

- boosts the immune system
- enhances rapid healing of minor wounds and injuries
- promotes cell repair
- rejuvenates body, mind and soul
- releases negative emotions
- tissue and organ healing

396 Hz: "*Inner peace*" frequency

- eliminates feelings of fear and guilt
- elimination of grief when struggling with a loss
- helps to turn grief into joy

417 Hz: "*New beginnings*" frequency

- can remove negative behavior patterns
- can reverse or undo negative experiences
- helpful when facilitating change
- removes negative energy from the body
- removes negative energy from the home or office

432 Hz: "*Peace and wellbeing*" frequency

- induces relaxation
- releases stress and tension from the body and mind
- slows your heart rate
- unites the body and mind with nature

528 Hz: "*Love*" frequency

- activates imagination
- awakens spirituality
- facilitates miracles and transformation
- focusses intention and intuition
- increases awareness

639 Hz: "*Harmony*" frequency

- builds positive energy

- helps repair turbulent friend, family or community relationships
- helps to connect with people on a deeper level
- increases understanding, empathy, tolerance and love
- promotes connection and harmony in relationships

741 Hz: *"Detox"* frequency
- awakens intuition
- helpful for those struggling with chronic pain
- improves problem solving
- provides mental clarity
- repels toxins and negative emotions

852 Hz: *"Enlightenment"* frequency
- deeper connection to your own consciousness
- enhances connection to the universe
- enhances spiritual enlightenment
- improves mental clarity and self-awareness
- reduces stress and anxiety
- stimulates intuition

963 Hz: *"God"* frequency
- can create room for oneness or unity with the spiritual world
- gateway to divine consciousness or enlightenment
- removes mental fog and brings clarity to your thoughts

Whether you believe it or not, even though the many health benefits associated with sound healing have been effectively utilized within numerous cultures and traditions over countless centuries, thankfully traditional Western medicine practices are finally beginning to see the light.

b) Schumann 7.83 Hz frequency
You may not be aware of this special, Extremely Low Frequency (ELF) and you may not know that it is also a relaxed alpha/theta brainwave frequency in your own brain. It's in this dreamy sleep state that cell regeneration and healing take place in your body.

Also called the "Schumann Resonance" (SR), discovered by Winfried Otto Schumann in 1952, this special 7.83 Hz frequency is the natural rhythm or heartbeat of our Mother Earth. Unfortunately, most of us are constantly living in a noisy world of organized chaos where we are subjected to a 24/7 bombardment of technology and endless confusing noise.

You are living in close contact with superficial wavelengths (cell phones and towers, telecommunication stations, microwave towers, network satellites, WIFI, computers, appliances and more), all of which are part of your everyday life, and all of which disrupt the natural healing (7.83 Hz) frequency of the Earth.

What this means for your health, especially if you live in a more heavily populated area, is that besides the air, light and noise pollution that you may not realize is having a detrimental effect on your life, you may find yourself living a life of chronic pain.

Ask yourself: ***"Am I feeling overly sensitive, irritated, angry, quick to react and overall unbalanced without really knowing why?"***

Stop to consider for a moment that the massive amounts of technology around you means that you are literally living under a cloud of frequencies that can range between 30,000 Hz and 300 billion Hz.

Knowing this, it's easy to understand why your own bio-electromagnetic waves might be out of balance and could be the cause of why you might be succumbing to any number of health issues, including the mysterious fibromyalgia.

You simply cannot deny that the natural frequency of the earth (7.83 Hz) is far, far lower than all the other created and potentially harmful frequencies that have become part of your daily life.

It's certainly not a far stretch to understand that while being out of balance with the earth's own magnetic frequency (7.83 Hz) would create emotional distress and other health-related problems, just as being in tune with the earth's frequency would help to heal and rejuvenate the body.

Thankfully, to escape from some of these harmful frequencies, or at least help yourself to feel more balanced and able to heal, there are many free, simple small steps you can take which are outlined in this book.

c) Sleep to healing music

You've already read about all the various Hz levels that you can listen to throughout your day to help with healing your mind and body.

What about all that time you spend sleeping? This is a perfect opportunity to take advantage of healing music. Not only will it help you to relax and get to sleep faster, but it can also help to heal you even when you're not consciously aware of it.

Playing relaxing music while you sleep helps to diminish exterior noise, block anxiety, overthinking, negative thoughts, and can even trigger the release of dopamine (the pleasure hormone) that can divert your thoughts away from pain so that you can sleep more peacefully.

There are now endless, peaceful sleep videos you can choose from designed for healing the mind and body while you sleep, so why not make healing sleep music a part of your new routine and enjoy a better sleep while healing your body at the same time?

During my fibro fight, I made sure that whenever possible, I would be listening to healing music, day and night, and I still do.

4. The Power of Laughter

You've no doubt heard that *"Laughter is the best medicine."* Is this just something people say, or is there truth that free laughter is very strong medicine?

"Laughter is an instant vacation."
~ Milton Berle ~

The good news is that yes, laughter is very good for your health. Besides just making you feel better when you laugh, that release of feel-good endorphins creates measurable health benefits:

- Boosts the immune system
- Can add years to your life
- Decreased high blood pressure
- Diminished pain
- Helps to connect with others
- Holds you in the present moment
- Improved mood
- Protects the heart
- Relaxes the entire body
- Relieves stress
- Shifts perspective
- Stimulates heart, lungs, muscles

Rather than spending your leisure time reading or watching all those terrifying, apocalyptic or murder movies that can cause stress and leave you feeling like the world is ending, choose to read or watch something that makes you smile, laugh and feel happy and optimistic about your future.

Instead of binge-watching serious, and often disturbing crime series on Netflix © or other entertainment mediums, why not find a funny comedy series to binge-watch and feel better?

It doesn't matter what makes you laugh. Whether it's movies or stories with happy endings, crazy cat videos, classic sitcoms or the joke of the day, there is no doubt that finding more ways to bring laughter into your life will definitely make you feel better, both mentally and physically.

Consider subscribing to a comedy channel or podcast online to get your daily feed of laughter therapy. Here's a few jokes to get you started.

Don't trust atoms
[They make up everything]

I named my toilet Jim instead of John. Everyone is so impressed when I tell them I go to the Jim every morning.

I just wrote a book on reverse psychology. Do not read it.

*I just did a course on positive thinking. It was sh*t.*

What happens when a frog's car breaks down?
[It gets toad]

5. Home Life Adjustment

In today's world, many of us live and work at home. No matter how much time you spend in your home environment, you may not be aware of all the very simple, free and highly effective changes you can make in your home environment that will really help you to feel better. But first . . .

"If you want to fly, give up everything that weighs you down."
~ Buddha ~

Before we begin, there is one adjustment in your home (especially if you also work there) that you may not have realized could be contributing to your feelings of unease or irritation and difficulty concentrating

a) Clear the clutter
Living and/or working in a space that is crowded with too much stuff can affect your health, and not in a good way! Living amidst a cluttered, messy home affects almost every system in your body because there is a

direct correlation between clutter and higher levels of stress hormones. In other words, the more clutter, the higher the stress.

Did you know that the average American household contains an amazing 300,000 items? If all this stuff is not neatly organized and put in its proper place, besides the excessive stimuli that makes it difficult to concentrate, too much clutter also invokes feelings of anxiety, frustration and guilt which then creates physical symptoms:

- Body Aches
- Disturbed sleep
- Feeling overwhelmed
- Feeling tired
- Headaches
- Increased blood pressure
- Lower self-esteem

If you are living and/or working in a space that is cluttered, here's a helpful quote for knowing what to keep and what to remove from your space:

"The first step in crafting the life you want is to get rid of everything you don't."

~ Joshua Becker ~

There is a meditation video on YouTube © titled: *"20 minute guided meditation for reducing anxiety and stress – Clear the clutter to calm down."* By The Mindful Movement. I used to listen to this, whilst resting on my bed, every day and it helped me a lot at the beginning of my recovery!

There are many small changes or adjustments you can make to your home life, that cost nothing and can help you feel better and work your way toward a fibro-free life.

b) Meditate

If I told my friends who I haven't seen for ages that I am doing meditation, they would not believe me and say: *"Not in a million years would you do meditation. You are not that kind of person!"* Those friends are not aware of my "*after-fibromyalgia-life.*" Meditation, just like healing music, was very important for me and helped me change, subconsciously, to be the person I am today: calm and content.

There are many health benefits scientifically proven to be associated with taking the time to meditate; see later in this book.

"You should sit in meditation for 20 minutes every day – Unless you're too busy. Then you should sit for an hour."
~ Zen proverb ~

I absolutely love that quote! It says so much!

While many may *"sit"* in a particular pose when meditating, most meditations can be done sitting or lying down, in your home, under a tree in your garden, or any place where you feel comfortable and able to slow your mind and be in the present moment.

Maybe you've always thought of meditation as a timely indulgence only practiced in earnest by Eastern religions seeking to attain inner peace. Perhaps you're completely sceptical and consider that silently sitting in cross-legged lotus pose while contemplating your navel is nothing more than an inconvenient waste of time, or a habit for the idle rich. That's what I *used* to think.

If this sounds like you, it may be time to take a closer look at what meditation really is, the different types of meditation, what type may be right for you, and how it can benefit you in many healthy ways.

Simply put, meditation is a technique to teach the mind to slow down enough to be aware of the present moment. Meditation has been in use for thousands of years, and in today's ultra-fast-paced world is a free self-help tool that is needed more than ever.

"Stop trying to calm the storm. Calm yourself and the storm will pass."
~ Buddha ~

While ancient in origin and included in many spiritual traditions, meditation does not belong to any specific faith or religion. In other words, all that you need to benefit from the practice of meditation is the desire to achieve better health by creating a sense of calm, peaceful harmony within yourself.

Types of meditation

There are many different types of meditation and many reasons why you might like to make meditation part of your new and improved health routine.

I have listed many popular types below, with a short explanation of what each style is concerned with, so that you can decide which type might be best for you.

Focused: involves focus on any of the 5 senses, such as counting your breath.

Loving-kindness: involves opening your mind to send and receive love from others, strengthen and nurture feelings of compassion and acceptance to yourself and all living beings.

Mantra: uses a repetitive sound, word or phrase to clear the mind (such as "om") and can be chanted loudly or softly over a period of time to help you become more alert and experience deeper levels of awareness.

Mindful: without judgment, paying attention to your thoughts as they enter your mind. Without becoming involved, simply observe and notice any patterns that may emerge. This is one of my favorite meditation types.

Movement: this is the simple act of completely focusing on the movement you are involved in, and really feeling every aspect of it, to develop body awareness, whether it be walking, showering, gardening, or other forms of gentle movement.

Progressive relaxation: involves tightening and relaxing muscle groups in your body to release stress and tension so that you can unwind and promote relaxation. I recommend you try this as it will transform you into a very relaxed state afterwards and can help you to fall asleep.

Self-love: often we are our own worst critics, and as such it may always be a good idea to practice a meditation that addresses being kinder to ourselves. A self-love meditation will help you to learn more about yourself, so that you can release any possible negative self-talk, which will help you to feel happier and more creative.

Spiritual: focuses on understanding religious or spiritual meaning and connection with a higher power.

Transcendental: usually taught by a practitioner, using a mantra to induce a state of calm and inner peace.

Visualization: focusses on increasing feelings of calm, peace and relaxation by visualizing figures, images or beautiful scenes and using all senses to imagine as much detail as possible.

Since this chapter is about helping to alleviate fibro pain on a small budget, I must point out that meditation costs nothing while being a simple tool for improved health that you can rely upon anywhere you might be, especially when it comes down to the anxiety and depression that tends to come hand in hand with chronic pain.

When you make a connection between your mind and your body, you have the power to improve your overall physical and mental health. Some of the proven health benefits of the simple, mindful practice of regular meditation include:

- Controlled food cravings
- Enhanced mood
- Improved brain health
- Improved focus
- Improved sleep
- Increased empathy and connection to others
- Increased self-confidence
- Lowered blood pressure
- May help to curb addictions
- Reduced anxiety and depression
- Reduced chronic pain
- Reduced inflammation
- Reduced stress

Guided meditation

There are meditation videos for just about everything online, from 5 minutes to 11 hours (to play during sleep): Healing Your Emotions, Stress, Self-love, Anxiety, Cluttered mind, Mental strength, Sleep, Healing during your sleep, Inner peace, etc.

In guided meditation a voice will give you instructions on what to do. This means that you have to listen to the voice and subsequently you will stay more "in the zone" without your mind wandering off to your "to-do list". I prefer guided meditation and find it extremely relaxing and helpful.

If you search online for "meditation", you will find a lot of videos either without a voice (just relaxing music) or with a voice only sporadically and the rest of the meditation is relaxing music. Search for "guided meditation" if you prefer to hear a voice most of the time during the meditation.

While 20 minutes meditating each day costs nothing and would be wonderfully beneficial for your health, a more realistic approach might be to begin with just 10 minutes every couple of days.

How to get started meditating (without guidance)
There is no definitive way to meditate, and you most certainly do not need to sit cross-legged on the floor, the following simple steps may help to get you started:

1) Find a comfortable position, either in a chair, on the couch or lying down (the key here is "comfortable")
2) Make sure you will not be disturbed during your meditation
3) Notice your breath and how it makes your abdomen rise and fall. If your mind begins to wander, again focus on your breath
4) Focus attention on your body. Note how each area of your body feels from your toes to top of your head.
5) If there are other sensations or feelings in your body, simply notice them, without judgements and return to focusing on your breathing

After you have become used to the sensation of shutting out the world by learning how to focus only on your breath or the sensations felt in your own body for 5 minutes, increase to 10, then 20.

Now you may be ready to experiment with any or all the different types of meditation types outlined above. There is no right or wrong way to meditate, so find the one that makes you feel the most relaxed and which removes distractions and disconnects you most effectively from the rest of the world that is constantly hammering to get in.

Important: Please don't tell yourself that meditation is not for you because "you don't believe in it" (negative signal to your brain). I suggest you try it for 2 or 3 weeks, every 2 days or so, and be **open** to how it might help you. You might be surprized. It did absolute wonders for me!

c) Take a nap
"Me? Taking a nap? Don't think so!" is what I would say if people suggested I have a day-nap. That was pre-fibro. During my fibro battle I was constantly exhausted and had 2 or 3 day-naps, which helped me recover. I still take naps on some days and no longer feel guilty to do so, which is a very large achievement for me, having been a workaholic.

Napping is not just for babies, retired folks who don't have a work schedule to adhere to any more or the elderly who have earned the right to do whatever they feel like, no matter the time of day.

"Napping – the only workout where you can wear pyjamas and still feel accomplished."
~ Unknown ~

The benefits of permitting yourself to take a nap in the middle of the day are quite substantial and there are many studies proving that there are quite a few nap benefits associated with this little indulgence.

A small nap mid-afternoon (between 1 and 3pm) can have big benefits, including improving your memory and job performance, making you more alert, easing stress, and improving your mood and creativity. Having a short nap when you need to study or power through some work can be much more effective than that cup of coffee to keep you going.

So how long is a *"small"* nap? Studies have shown that the most optimum length of time for an afternoon nap is about 10 to 30 minutes. Apparently any longer than 30 minutes, the longer it will take to shake the nap grogginess so that you can wake up and get back to work.

d) Dead sea salt

The Dead Sea (in Israel), although not a sea at all, is the deepest and saltiest lake in the world that has been renowned for its mineral rich healing properties since Biblical times. Being ten times saltier than any ocean means that it is naturally rich in bromide, calcium, magnesium, and potassium. The Dead Sea is considered to be one of the very first naturally occurring *"health resorts."*

Known as nature's *"fountain of youth"*, soaking for 10 to 20 minutes in a bath containing a cup of Dead Sea salt offers many health enhancing benefits that you can enjoy in your own home, such as:

- Deep hydration – calcium and magnesium attract and hold water to support the skin's water balance and alleviate dry skin.
- Exfoliation and cleansing – with natural antibacterial properties, the salt cleans and exfoliates the surface of your skin to reveal a healthy new layer.
- Healing chronic skin conditions – it has been proven that anyone suffering from psoriasis or dry, itchy skin will benefit greatly.
- Soothes sore muscles – anti-inflammatory and detoxing, promotes relaxation by soothing painful joints and muscles, swelling, stiffness and cramps. A Dead Salt bath is very good for muscle pain with fibromyalgia.
- Youthful skin – the minerals fight off oxidation by eliminating free radicals that lead to aging.

As well as improving skin conditions and being an effective way to unwind after a busy day, soaking in sea salt is known to improve more significant health concerns, including inflammatory arthritic diseases as well as autoimmune diseases that can cause your immune system to attack your bones, joints, muscles, and organs.

All the above is certainly a relaxing and easy way to improve your aches and pains, so why wouldn't you want to try it? If a bath is not on the cards for you, you can still gain the benefits by simply having a Dead Sea salt foot soak.

My personal experience is much pain relief, a feeling of deep relaxation and a much more restful sleep after a Dead Sea salt soak, all of which are often difficult to achieve when you're suffering from fibromyalgia.

An Epsom Salt (containing magnesium) bath also has many health benefits, especially for your muscles.

e) Limit phone and computer time
Just because the phone rings, or you hear a text message coming in does not mean that you have to rush to answer it or reply, especially if this means being interrupted from that 5-minute meditation break you were in the middle of.

"Dance like nobody is watching, because they're not – they're busy checking their phones."
~ Unknown ~

Here's an idea – leave your phone at home and go for a walk in the woods, or drive to the seashore, away from technology, with no distractions apart from the sound of birds and wind rattling the leaves in the treetops or the sound of seagulls and crashing waves.

If the thought of leaving home without your phone causes you to experience anxiety or a full-blown panic attack, perhaps rather than technology helping you through your day, you need to question how much technology may be damaging your health.

Overuse of technology (smartphone and Internet addiction), besides causing eye strain, poor posture, back pain, neck pain, wrist pain, headaches, insomnia, diabetes, obesity and premature death, is known to cause anxiety, and depression. Further, the constant interruption creates difficulty focusing on other aspects of your life.

Rather than subjecting yourself to information overload and spending your entire day behind your phone or computer screen, set a timer and get up every hour to move and stretch and do something that has absolutely nothing to do with a computer, texting or social media.

I spent a lifetime behind a computer screen for 10+ hours each day, barely moving, totally immersed in what I was doing, and I can tell you from personal experience that this workaholic attitude was a large factor in having created my own health issues.

f) Socialize with friends and family
You need to get out there, despite your pains, and socialize with other people, because living a life of isolation and keeping to yourself will only make you feel that much worse.

I was very surprized when I occasionally went out with friends when I had a lot of pain as I realized when I was back home that during my socializing time, I didn't have as many pains as usual. The clear reason for this is that my mind was not concentrating on my pain. Instead, my brain was receiving positive messages of the enjoyment I was experiencing being with my friends.

It's very important to maintain your social support network when you're experiencing daily pain in your life. When navigating our busy lives, we often forget about how important it is to take the time to socialize and keep in touch with our friends and family who are a lifeline that reminds us that we are not alone and who can help us to recall past moments of happiness and joy or create new ones.

Getting together with friends is an opportunity to forget about your aches and pains, feel happier in the moment and let your mind explore and plan for all the possibilities of joyful moments that the future will bring.

"All work and no play makes Jack a dull boy"

This very old saying, of course, can be equally applied to any gender and simply means that a person who never takes time off to enjoy friends, family get-togethers, or the simpler things in life is not only bored, but actually becomes boring themselves.

Developing and maintaining relationships that include close family and true friends you can really talk to about how you're feeling doesn't just make your life more enjoyable, it also has an important, positive impact on your day-to-day health and wellbeing.

Besides life being meant for good friends and great adventures, true friends are simply good for your health for many reasons, including that they:

- Decrease pain levels
- Encourage a positive attitude

- Encourage healthy habits
- Encourage you to try new things
- Help you cope
- Help you live longer
- Improve your self-confidence
- Increase your happiness
- Increase your sense of belonging
- Increase your sense of purpose
- Prevent mental decline
- Reduce anxiety
- Reduce depression
- Reduce high blood pressure
- Reduce your stress

As you can clearly see, the benefits of maintaining the support of close friendships with people you care about are widespread and a definite win/win for both sides of the relationship.

If you have been allowing fibromyalgia to keep you away from your friends, it's time to realize the health benefits of maintaining these important relationships and get back in touch, because:

"If you have good friends, no matter how much life is sucking, they can make you laugh."
~ P.C. Cast ~

If you don't have any friends or family, consider joining online websites e.g. social media fibromyalgia groups or chat groups. You will then realize that you are not alone with this horrible illness. Other people can encourage you, give you some tips and maybe make you feel better.

g) Limit the time you sit

I am talking here about limiting the time you sit when you are **not** on your computer. The newest catch phrase that you've more than likely heard someone say these days is: *"Sitting is the new smoking."* Of course, this is a less than subtle way of telling you to get off your butt if you don't want to prematurely shorten your life.

Your body is not designed for lazy living, it is designed to **move**. Therefore, if you are finding yourself locked into a sedentary lifestyle, for your health's sake, and as part of your regimen to give fibro the finger, it's time to change this habit and find ways to get moving again.

"Life always begins with one step outside of your comfort zone."
~ Shannon L. Alder ~

h) Cold showers

I found that in the beginning of my fibro battle cold showers worked very well for me. There are many benefits when you take a cold shower:

- Builds willpower as it takes a lot of will power to take a cold shower. Each time you turn the tap to colder and colder and colder, your willpower is increased.
- Combats depressive symptoms
- Improves circulation
- Improves hair and skin for many people
- Reduces inflammation
- Reduces muscle soreness
- Trains your nervous system so that you will become more resilient to stress

Make sure to start with a medium cold shower and increase the cold every 2 days or so until you have reached your limit of "coldness." If a cold shower is not for you, why not give these a try:

- Simply hold your hands under the tab and run cold water over your wrists for 1 to 3 minutes. The cold water runs over your main vain and subsequently through your whole body.
- Run cold water in the bath, up to your knees or just below your knees. Stand in the cold water with your feet. Start with 1 minute and work up to 10 minutes. This was surprisingly very helpful for me.

i) Pet power

Perhaps you've already heard that simply petting your cat or dog, or spending time caring for any other type of furred, feathered or scaled friend can decrease your stress hormone (cortisone) and lower your blood pressure. Of course, while this is true, caring for a pet of your own can be expensive.

However, there are also many people who would be happy to let you walk their dog or look after their dog while they are away so that you can experience the health benefits at no cost to you. You could take this on as a part-time job and improve your health **and** earn a bit of money at the same time.

There are many other, far reaching physical and mental health benefits that have been scientifically proven, when caring for a pet that you may not have considered:

- Distraction from distressing symptoms
- Fewer allergies
- Improved fitness

- Improved heart health
- Improved mood
- Less anxiety
- Less depression
- Lowered blood pressure
- Lowered cholesterol
- Reduced pain and discomfort
- Reduced risk of diabetes
- Reduced risk of stroke and cancer
- Stronger bones
- Stronger immune system

As you can see, besides a happier outlook and an overall improved quality of life that is part of caring for a pet, just being around them brings many smiles and literally helps you to live longer and stay healthier. Caring for a pet also takes the focus off yourself, nurtures social connections and gives you the motivation to take better care of yourself, so that you can take better care of them.

j) Plan a long break

I used to be proud to say to friends, co-workers or clients that I worked 7-days a week (often long into the night) and had not taken a holiday or a real break from work for ten years, which before long increased to fifteen and more years.

Now I say, ***"I need a break so long, that I forget all my passwords!"***

It took literally a world of pain before I realized that working every day of the week, and never giving myself permission to take a long break was nothing to be proud of. It was a hard pill to swallow when I finally realized that I had greatly contributed to my own declining health.

If you work at home, or run your own business, where it's easy to work longer than the standard 7 or 8 hours you would work if you commuted to an outside work environment every day, or have workaholic tendencies, do yourself a favor and take the weekends off from work and enjoy fun outings and share time with friends and family over relaxing long weekends.

A holiday doesn't have to be luxurious or expensive as you could even have a tent-holiday somewhere in a field or a caravan holiday on special offer. You could just stay at home for a week and practice some methods to calm your mind, take a nap, go for walks, etc. Whatever you fancy doing, as long as you change your daily stressful routine.

Never taking a break and working 24/7 is nothing to be proud of and can put you on a path toward risking having many painful health issues.

6. Take a Breath

It's time to learn how to breathe. I know, you're saying, *"What are you talking about? I'm breathing all day long."*

Of course you are, however, there's a very big difference between the shallow breath that keeps you alive day and night and intentionally focusing on peaceful, relaxing deep breathing. Studies have shown that being mindful and learning to focus on controlling your breath is beneficial in stress management and any stress-related conditions, such as fibromyalgia pain.

Here's an interesting fact about diaphragmatic breathing. The diaphragm is a muscle, located below the lungs, to help you breathe in and out. When you were born you were naturally engaging the diaphragm to take deep, refreshing breaths. As you get older, unless you are a trained singer, your breathing pattern gradually shifts to shallower chest breathing.

Because you used to know how to breathe through the diaphragm, this probably helps now as you are re-learning how to do this type of health-promoting belly breathing that encourages full oxygen exchange.

There are many beneficial physical and mental effects that occur when you take a break from the rest of your day and focus on purposeful deep breathing. It costs nothing, can be done anywhere, at any time, doesn't take a long time (just a few minutes), and besides being relaxing, the benefits to your health are:

- Alleviates post-traumatic stress disorder
- Improves heart health
- Improves immune system
- Improves sleep
- Reduces anxiety
- Reduces depression
- Reduces hypertension
- Reduces stress
- Relieves pain
- Sharpens memory

There are lots of free videos online about diaphragmatic breathing.

While being mindful of your breathing is a form of meditation (discussed earlier), and there are many techniques, mindful breathing can easily be practiced on its own.

Which breathing technique is best? There are many deep breathing techniques, and you may wish to try them all. The best one is the one that works well for you. The following 2 are simple breathing formulas to get you started.

1-count longer breathing exercise

1) Breathe slowly in through the nose, hold your breath and count slowly to 4.
2) Then breathe out through the mouth and breathe out for 5 slow counts.
3) Breathe from the belly (diaphragm), not the chest. Place a hand on your belly button and feel it rise and fall.

You can also count to 5 when holding your breath and count to 6 when exhaling. Your exhale must be 1 second longer than your inhale.

4-7-8 Breathing exercise

Andrew Weil, MD, created this technique, he termed this procedure a "natural nervous system tranquilizer." This is how to it:

1) Sit or lie down and place one palm on your stomach. Shut your eyes.
2) Put your tongue's tip behind your top front teeth. Keep it there for the duration of the exercise.
3) Close your mouth and inhale through your nostrils to the slow count of 4.
4) Hold your breath for 7 slow counts.
5) Open your mouth and exhale through it for 8 slow counts, generating a whooshing sound.
6) Repeat it three times daily.

Once you are familiar with these simple relaxation techniques and are beginning to enjoy the feeling of deep relaxation every time you take a few minutes for a breath break, you will always have a secret weapon. You can use this weapon any time you need a moment to relax and recharge before you head back into your busy day. You'll soon be enjoying all the many health benefits.

7. Food Choices

Talking about food choices is not exactly everyone's favorite topic because we all know that sometimes we don't make the best choices about what we put inside our bodies.

"After a good dinner, one can forgive anybody, even one's own relatives."

~ Oscar Wilde ~

Most of us have a list of foods that we regularly consume that we know aren't the best choices for our health, but we continue to eat them anyway because they make us feel good (so we think), and we're addicted.

a) Junk food addiction

Most processed fast foods are high in sugar and fat (or both) and cause blood sugar imbalances, which makes you crave them.

"Junk food isn't cheap. We pay a steep price for it, years after consuming it."

~ Joel Furhman ~

Often these less-than-optimal foods fall under the category of *"fast foods"* or snacks that are high in calories and loaded with salt and sugar, which just makes you want to eat more of them.

While some junk food may have limited food value, for the most part, it's just easier to consider that junk food is anything that has no nutritional value. I like to call this *"empty calories."*

An empty calorie junk food will almost certainly taste good, because junk food is literally engineered to make you crave it, overeat it, and think about how you can get more of it as often as possible.

Whether you call junk food *"empty calories", "processed", "pre-packaged"* or simply *"food of low nutritional value",* the word "JUNK" is a big tip off that eating it is not good for your health.

The Webster dictionary meaning for the word *"junk"* includes:

- Secondhand, worn or discarded
- Something of little meaning, worth or significance
- Something of poor quality
- Something to get rid of as worthless

The junk food industry is really helping to drive the obesity epidemic. Besides all the extra weight that most of society can do without, it's pretty obvious that you should not eat junk food, so why do so many have difficulty giving it up?

Unfortunately, despite the health hazards eating junk food poses, selling it is big business and because of this the dollar hungry food industry has spared no cost in designing and flooding the shelves with items that are the perfect combination of artificial flavor, fat, salt, and sugar that triggers very powerful reward signals in your brain.

Every time you eat one of these specially manufactured, highly rewarding, feel-good snacks, dopamine spikes occur and instruct your brain to repeat this rewarding sensation by eating more. This is why when you're feeling unhappy, eating junk food seems to make you feel better.

The secret to kicking the junk food habit is to find real foods that satisfy just as much and are easy to make out of high-quality, real food ingredients.

To explain this in detail is beyond the scope of this book. If you need help with this, rather than beating yourself up about it, just go online and ask for help learning how to turn junk food cravings into healthy eating habits. This will not only make you feel better, but it will also make you healthier and happy about taking good care of your body.

b) Sugar addiction

Despite what we know about the harmful health effects of eating a diet high in sugar, avoiding it is much easier said than done. Sugar is becoming more and more difficult to avoid because it's part of your DNA to like it, it's found everywhere, it's in almost everything, and it's highly addictive.

Here's a scary fact: the average person eats approximately 17 teaspoons of sugar every day, when ideally, we are told that this should be between 6 and 9. That's 2-3 times more than the recommended amount!

Before we discuss ways to avoid eating too much sugar, let's first list some of the important reasons why you need to make an effort to reduce this sweet intake, because too much sugar can put you at higher risk for:

- Cardiovascular disease
- Cavities and tooth decay
- Chromium deficiency
- Colon cancer
- Compromised immune function
- Diabetes
- Gum disease
- High blood pressure

- Increased stress
- Inflammation
- Kidney disease
- Liver disease
- Muscle & nerve damage
- Obesity
- Pancreatic cancer
- Retina damage
- Skin aging and wrinkles
- Unstable blood sugar

That's a long hit list of serious health issues that can be attributed to consuming too much sugar and many of these can also contribute to fibromyalgia pain.

In case you were in any doubt about how harmful sugar can be to your health, you will want to read this list several times over and hopefully will be motivated to take action to do something about reducing your intake.

I find the easiest way to reduce sugar intake is to go *"cold turkey."* Just a little sugar weakens your resolve, and it becomes too easy to slide into just a little more as those feel-good dopamine spikes take over.

Seemingly innocuous sugar can certainly be a big player in your fight against many chronic diseases, including fibromyalgia. Think seriously before drinking that soda or putting that donut in your mouth, and ask yourself, ***"Is eating this food going to help me in my fight against fibro?"***

How can you reduce your daily intake of sugar? The first step is simply being aware of how much sugar you may be eating daily. If you're ready to get some of the sugar out of your life, here are a few tips to help get you started:

- Buy plain yogurt and sweeten with fresh fruit or a touch of honey
- Dilute 100% fruit juice with ¾ water
- Ditch the soda (hydrate with water and a little lemon)
- Make fresh fruit your *"go to"* for a sweet snack
- Read the labels (5% is a little, 15% or more is a lot)
- Wean yourself off adding sugar to tea or coffee
- When baking, substitute sugar for banana, applesauce, dried fruit

Once you get started, you will find many more ways you can actively reduce your daily sugar intake and kick the sugar habit. Less sugar means less inflammation, and that translates to less pain in your life.

When you were young, it felt like you could eat pretty much all the junk food you wanted and not suffer any concerning side effects. The reason you could get away with this when you were young was because you were much more active, your immune system was strong, and you had not yet suffered from a lifetime of choosing to consume less than optimal foods.

However, when you continue to eat foods that are not optimum choices for your best health, you are making it more difficult for yourself to feel better. Being aware of this simple fact and deciding to do something about it can go a long way toward helping to heal fibro pain.

Take some time to go through your cupboards and see if there is a lot of food you've been eating that may have contributed to a toxic overload and a less than healthy body and choose to get rid of them.

c) Diet choices
As I'm certain you are aware, there are many different choices when it comes to deciding what type of diet may be the best one for you, the key is finding one that works well enough for you that you are encouraged to stick with it.

"My doctor told me to stop having intimate dinners for four. Unless there were three other people."
~ Orson Welles ~

While you may experiment with several different diet types before deciding which one works best for you, apparently, the 5 most common diet choices these days, that are supported by science, include:

Gluten-free: this type of diet came into being because of those who were intolerant to the gluten found in barley, rye and wheat and crossed over to those who wanted to lose weight by removing carbohydrates from their diet.

Low-carbohydrate, whole food: this diet is low in starches, sugar and processed food, while being high in vegetables, meat, fish, eggs, fruits, nuts, and fats.

Mediterranean: this type of diet focuses on food common to the Mediterranean region, such as extra virgin olive oil, fruits, vegetables, dairy, fish, poultry, legumes and whole grains.

Paleo: this recently popular diet choice is so named because it focuses on unprocessed foods that were eaten by our paleolithic ancestors.

Vegan: this is a diet that excludes all animal products in favor of being exclusively plant-based.

Now you're wondering which one of the above diets I chose to follow as I was strategically eliminating fibromyalgia from my life. The answer to that question is, *"None of the above."*

Carnivore diet

I chose a Carnivore diet path that most might think is a big step outside of the box because it was in total contradiction to everything I had been taught about eating a healthy diet as a child and everything I had learned over the past 5 decades about all the many diets, each of which professed to be the best.

How did I come to embrace what most would consider a radical diet choice? A large and very compelling influence for me was a video by Dr. Anthony Chaffee *("Plants are Trying to Kill You!")* that was sent to me by a friend who knew that I was suffering with fibromyalgia. Dr. Chaffee is an American medical doctor who: *"Over a span of 20+ years has researched the optimal nutrition for human performance and health."* His video really made complete sense to me and after watching it, I was eager to embark on this new diet plan.

Please note: I am not advocating any particular type of diet and am certainly not trying to convince you that you should follow my diet plan, because what I chose may not be the best choice for you. I am merely sharing my personal experience with the Carnivore diet, which I believe to be one of the best things I have ever done for my health.

I noticed almost an immediate reduction in my daily pain when I completely stopped eating vegetables, fruits, and grains and instead ate only meat, fish, eggs, and some dairy. While extremely restrictive, I could not deny how much better I felt.

The carnivore diet (also known as a zero-carb diet) is simply a diet that excludes all plant-based foods in favor of consuming only foods that used to fly, swim or walk.

I also continued to take a full spectrum of vitamins, and after about 2 months I fine-tuned my carnivore diet to include approximately 10% of targeted nutrients including a small amount of blackberries and blueberries. These are high in antioxidants. I added bioflavonoids found in black currants and green citrus fruit to my diet and a small amount of sunflower and pumpkin seeds.

No matter what diet choices you decide to make, most would agree that the more sugar (especially in processed forms) that you can omit from your diet, the greater your chances of eliminating the inflammatory pains often associated with fibromyalgia that are known to be the result of consuming a diet high in sugar.

8. The Power of Intermittent Fasting

While intermittent fasting may not be for everyone, it's not as scary as it might sound because it doesn't mean starving yourself for days. If you are determined to feel better, you may find that intermittent fasting could very well be particularly helpful. Check with your health care provider first.

"Intermittent" simply means that you would choose to not eat for approximately 12 hours each day. This is quite easy to do if you stop eating at 6:00 pm (go to sleep for 7 or 8 hours) and don't eat again until 12 hours later (6:00 am).

The above is my preferred intermittent fasting method, and I found this always made me feel better. If intermittent fasting sounds like something you would like to try, and it makes more sense for your schedule to block out a time during the day for not eating, don't forget to drink plenty of fluids (water, herbal tea, etc.).

Beyond currently being touted as the latest weight loss fad, fasting and intermittent fasting is nothing new because it has been used to help manage chronic conditions and heal the body since ancient times.

"The best of all medicines is resting and fasting."
~ Benjamin Franklin ~

Giving your body a rest from food may provide many other health benefits:

- Decreased risk of diabetes
- Improved brain function
- Improved detoxification
- Improved sleep
- Loss of visceral fat
- Lowered blood pressure
- Lowered cholesterol
- Reduced inflammation
- Reduced risk of cancer

- Reduced risk of cardiovascular events
- Slowed aging
- Stabilized blood sugar

As this chapter is about recovery on a small budget, it is important to mention some low-cost myofascial pain release tools other than the foam roller.

9. Myofascial Release at Low Cost

Below are the low-cost myofascial release tools I bought. Knowing that much of fibro pain could be attributed to tight fascia pulling everything out of alignment, I purchased a foam roller (discussed in chapter 1), balls and other rollers and they all worked!

a) Balls and rollers

I bought these balls: "*Top 3 Massage Balls Set* [$25 CAD, $18.30 USD, or £14.90], Spiky, Lacrosse ball, Peanut Muscle Roller Massager. Available on Amazon. (Prices were correct at time of printing)

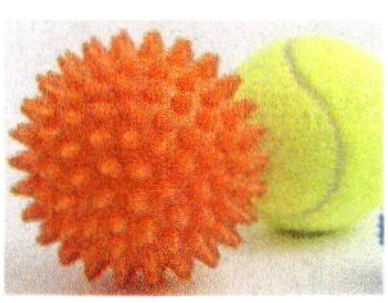

Spiky ball

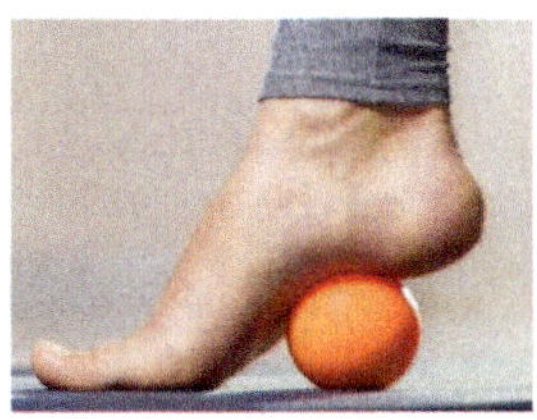

Lacrosse ball

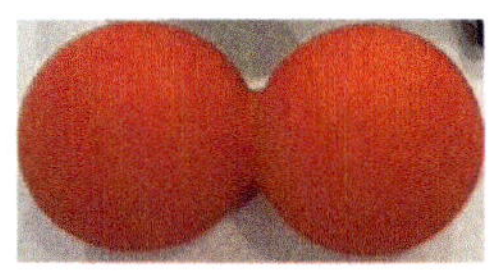

Peanut muscle roller

The ball set comes with a spiky ball, a lacrosse ball and a peanut muscle roller and I found these massage balls to be very helpful for locating and reducing painful spots anywhere on the body. I use the lacrosse ball for rolling under my feet, for just a few minutes while standing at my desk. I also roll the ball on the soles of my feet first thing in the morning and before bed at night.

Instead of buying a peanut muscle roller you could also put 2 tennis balls in a sock which will do the same job.

You can use the peanut roller to put each ball either side of your spine and lean against the wall and roll from the top of your spine to the bottom. You can also do this whilst lying on the floor on your back and roll your body up and down.

Never roll directly on your spine.

Balls are very portable and easy to use in many different scenarios, and you can use any type of soft ball that is approximately 3.93" (10 cm) or smaller in diameter (tennis ball, squash ball, racket ball). As an example, while lying on the floor, you can position the ball on a painful trigger point, breathe into it, and soon the pain diminishes. I found that the peanut muscle roller ball worked best for me on larger muscle groups and was especially helpful in reducing low back pain as the 2 smaller balls fit either side of the spine.

I purchased the "*Manual Massage Roller Ball*" [$12.50 CAD, $9.10 USD, or £7.45]. Available on Amazon. (Prices were correct at time of printing)

I also really like this roller ball because it's portable, a nice size that is easy to hold in the hand and the ball rolls easily and is large to quickly massage longer groups of muscles in the legs and arms. Also, if you're lucky enough to have a partner that doesn't mind assisting, this roller ball is also great for a back massage. This was an effective and economic purchase for me.

Rolling with a ball under your foot is a good way to heal but also to prevent pains as the foot has lots of pressure points that correlate with all parts of the body. You can use a tennis ball or any other plastic ball.

Rolling a ball on the bottom of the foot helps with back pain (including sciatica) and foot pain. Put your foot on the ball and gently apply pressure and push the ball into the floor. Move your foot and roll the ball back and forth from your toes to your heels. Do this for 1 to 2 minutes. Repeat on other foot. Do foot-rolling 3 to 4 times per week.

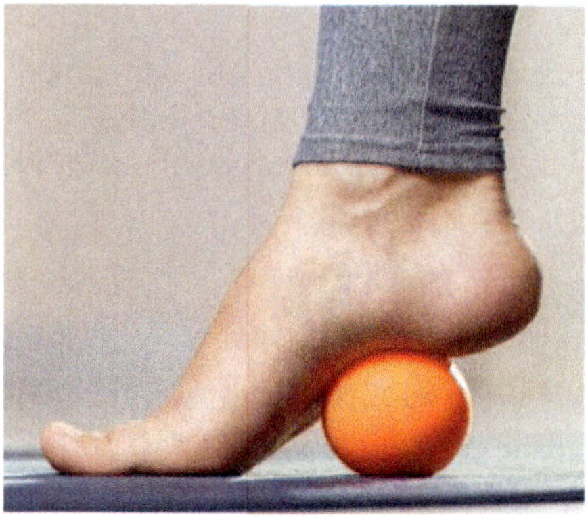

How to do myofascial release with balls: let the body-part you are releasing sink into the ball, use proprioception (so think about the body part in your mind), stay on the ball for 1 to 2 minutes or until you feel a release. **Slowly** roll up and down and/or left and right and hold still on tender spots. You can also just lie on the ball for up to 2 minutes without moving.

A few positions you can do with a ball (it doesn't have to be a spiky ball as shown on the picture):

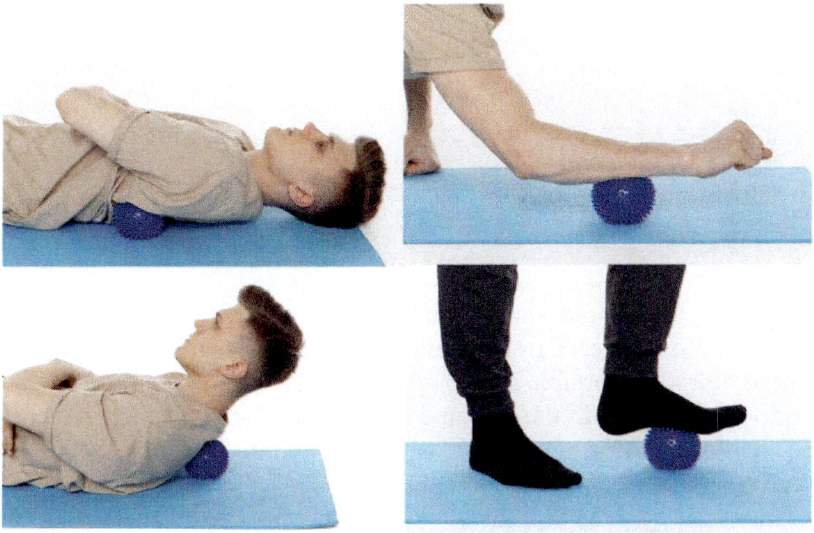

b) Other tools
The 2 last items I bought:

"Coolife Fascia Blasting Muscle Roller [$23.50 CAD, $17.20 USD, or £13.71*]*. Available on Amazon. (Prices were correct at time of printing)

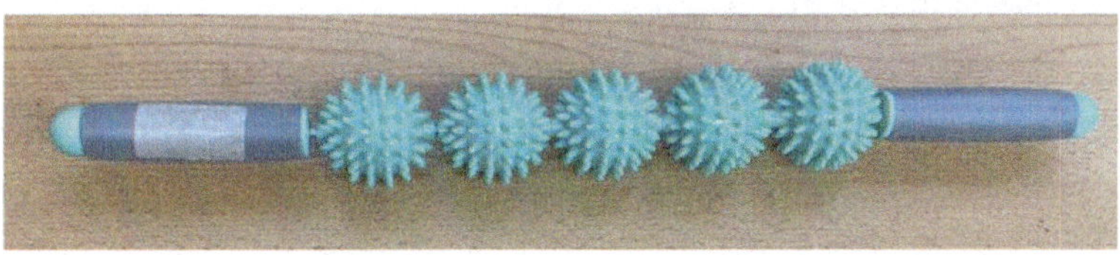

This roller works deep into the tight fascia and I only use it on tight areas I couldn't release with the balls. I use this mostly on my legs and calves whilst sitting down. At first this spiky roller feels quite intense. However, once you get used to the feeling of all those little spikes rolling over your muscle groups with just the right amount of pressure, and you relax into it, this massage stick tool really does a great job of releasing tight fascia.

"Fascia Muscle Roller" [$18.50 CAD, $13.50 USD, or £10.73*]*. Available on Amazon. (Prices were correct at time of printing)

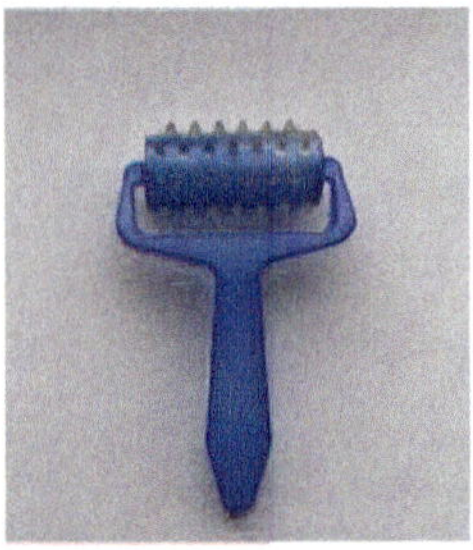

This roller is easy to hold, moves smoothly and has rows of raised bumps that help to release tight fascia without being painful. It's small enough to be easily portable and tough enough to do a great job on larger, longer muscles in the legs and arms or easy for a partner to use on the back. I used this one every day and found it to be quite effective at relieving soreness and pain.

After reading this chapter, you know lots of free (or very low cost) methods to help reduce your fibro pain or to make your fascia healthier. All it takes is a desire to help yourself and a commitment to taking the time to pursue them.

When you put your mind to it, I'm sure you can think of other free or low-cost therapies that could be very healing.

Chapter 9: Pills, Potions and Paraphernalia

This chapter starts with an overview of the types of medications traditionally prescribed for fibromyalgia pain. Followed by more expensive potions and devices that I have purchased and tested.

There are many options these days for medical intervention when it comes to pain relief. I have outlined what pain killers, vitamins, alternative potions and equipment that I've used, to help make my days bearable.

"When I was growing up, they used to say, 'Robin, drugs can kill you.' Now that I'm 58 my doctor's telling me, 'Robin, you need drugs to live.' I realize now that my doctor is also a dealer..."
~ Robin Williams ~

1. Pills

As I was self-medicating, this section is about the pain killers and vitamins I personally relied upon to help get me through my most painful fibro days.

During your time with fibro, make sure that you carry out extensive research and talk to your health care provider before engaging in any self-medicating program. This is especially important if you have other medical issues and are already taking medications for whatever reason because there may be unwanted side effects associated with mixing your medications and other pills.

Please note that the names of any medications listed in this book may be known under a different name, depending upon the country (i.e. USA, Canada, UK, Europe, etc.).

What are NSAID's? This is an abbreviation meaning *"Non-Steroidal Anti-Inflammatory Drugs"*, and they are commonly available and widely used to lower a high temperature, reduce inflammation and relieve pain.

There are many NSAIDs. Some of the more commonly recognized ones are Ibuprofen (sold under trade names Advil, Motrin, Nurofen and others) and Naproxen (sold under trade names Aleve, Naprosyn and others).

What are Opioids? These are very serious pain killers (narcotics), that require a prescription and are considered dangerous and highly addictive, whether made from the poppy plant or synthesized in a laboratory. Over-use of opioids can lead to life-threatening problems.

What are Corticosteroids? These are a type of man-made, anti-inflammatory drugs typically prescribed to treat rheumatological health issues, such as rheumatoid arthritis. For example, Prednisone is the most used corticosteroid.

What is an Anti-Inflammatory Analgesic? These are taken to relieve mild to moderate pain, without putting you to sleep, by reducing inflammation at the source. The most common analgesics are Aspirin (Acetylsalicylic acid) and Tylenol (Acetaminophen).

What is Paracetamol? Antipyretic (used to reduce fever) and analgesic agents are mostly used to help with fever and moderate pain. Paracetamol does not contain Opioids.

What are OTC Medications? OTC is an abbreviation for Over the Counter and simply means pain medications that you can purchase without a prescription at your local pharmacy or at many grocery stores, such as Advil (Ibuprofen), which is categorized as an NSAID or Tylenol (*Acetaminophen*), which is categorized as an Analgesic.

For example, although I was not taking any prescribed medications, I was lucky enough to have a good friend point out to me that prolonged use of my first choice of over the counter (OTC) pain medication (Advil) could cause liver damage if taken very often. Without realizing that taking Advil daily could be harmful to my liver, I had chosen a daily dose because it had previously always been effective for reducing my headache pain. I reduced my Advil over time until I no longer needed to take it.

I found it interesting that the Arthritis Foundation says that: *"Drugs such as NSAID's, opioids and corticosteroids have not been found to be effective for fibromyalgia pain"* because my personal experience has taught me otherwise.

2. FDA Approved for Fibromyalgia

There are currently several Federal and Drug Administration-approved medications commonly prescribed specifically for treatment of fibromyalgia pain. These include:

Duloxetine (*Cymbalta, Yentreve*) is an oral drug prescribed to treat **anxiety** and **major depressive disorder** and for the relief of nerve pain.

Some of the side effects attributed to taking Duloxetine include *diarrhea, mood swings, headache, sleep changes and feelings similar to electric shock.*

I asked myself: *"Why would someone already suffering from these types of pain want to take a drug that is known to cause them?"* The answer I think is simple: desperation or lack of knowledge.

Milnacipran (*Savella, Ixel, Dalcipran, Toledomin*) is an anti-depressant drug used to treat **depression** and for pain that affects the ligaments, muscles, tendons and supporting tissues.

The most frequently occurring side effects of taking Milnacipran include *mood swings, headache, insomnia, nausea, constipation and elevated blood pressure*. Again, many of these side effects are known to be symptoms of fibromyalgia.

Pregabalin (*Lyrica, Alzain, Axalid*) is a drug prescribed for the treatment of **anxiety**, nerve pain and to control epileptic seizures.

Some of the known side effects associated with taking Pregabalin include *headaches, mood changes, dizziness, diarrhea, nausea, memory problems, and suicidal thoughts*. Do I need to say it again?

Zolpidem (*Ambien, Edluar, Intermezzo, Zolpimist*) is a hypnotic oral drug (or spray) prescribed for the treatment of insomnia to help you fall asleep and/or stay asleep.

While there are many known side-effects that can be attributed to taking Zolpidem, several are also known to be fibromyalgia symptoms (*headache, diarrhea, tiredness, and muscle pain).*

I was very fortunate to be able to control my pain symptoms with Tylenol every day, and therefore cannot comment on the efficacy of any of the FDA medications (above) that are approved for fibromyalgia, beyond what their side effects may entail.

It seems that the medical community, while now being careful not to clearly state it, remains convinced that anyone suffering from fibromyalgia needs to be treated with drugs that are prescribed for 2 types of mental health disorders:

- Anxiety
- Depression

The American Psychological Association describes depression as being: ***"The most common mental disorder."***

When this chronic pain condition first reared its ugly head and was labelled fibromyalgia back in the late 1960's many medical practitioners were previously convinced that the *"fibrositis"* symptoms were an imagined mental disorder.

It is my opinion that while the medical community may now acknowledge that fibromyalgia is a real, chronic syndrome, for the most part, they are still treating it like a mental disorder.

3. What About Vitamin Pills?

In my search for pain relief I also chose to add various vitamins and spices to my diet, many of which are known to be potent antioxidants that are also helpful in reducing inflammation, including:

- Cayenne Pepper – lots of antioxidants, pain relief, digestive health
- Cinnamon – antioxidants, anti-inflammatory, lower blood sugar
- Ginger – antioxidants, increases happiness hormones, anxiety
- Green Tea – antioxidants, improve cognitive function
- Omega 3 Fatty Acids – functioning of all cells in your body
- Quercetin – antioxidants, anti-inflammatory, control blood sugar
- Turmeric Curcumin - antioxidants, anti-inflammatory, arthritis
- Vitamin B12 – tiredness, body's nerve cells and blood
- Vitamin D – helps body absorb calcium, control infections

While I cannot definitively report that the daily use of the above list made a noticeably significant difference in reducing my pain, they are all potent antioxidants that we can all benefit from in our battle against harmful free radicals that can seriously harm your health.

In today's nutritionally depleted world, taking daily supplements can provide peace of mind, because you are giving your body extra protection, and peace of mind means less stress.

Important note: some vitamins counteract each other so make sure you do your research on this topic.

4. Potions

Always having been an *"out of the box"* type of person who has avoided using any sort of standard drug regimen for my entire life, I began searching for alternative pain relief solutions so that I would not have to rely on taking my once-a-day analgesic.

"Don't panic – it's organic!"
~ Victoria B. Allen ~

a) CBD oil

Note: CBD and CB2 products are expensive but what exactly is the price of being pain free and being happy? Nobody knows the answer to this question. I don't have a huge amount of residual income, but I am very happy to drink less coffee in my favorite coffee shop or dine out less frequently so I can afford to pay for some aids so I can be pain free.

The first natural *"potion"* claiming to have great pain-relieving properties was in great abundance and easy to find pretty much anywhere. This was CBD, which stands for *"Cannabidiol"* and is the second most active ingredient in cannabis (marijuana). The first most active ingredient in the marijuana plant (the one that produces a high) is THC, which stands for *"TetraHhydroCannabinol"*.

While it has become legal in some countries to use and even grow your own recreational marijuana, I have never had any interest in using even a completely organic psychoactive product to alter my perception of the world. However, I was willing to test CBD because it promised pain relief without the high.

My first foray into the world of CBD products began with the purchase of a bottle of organic CBD THC-free oil which stated on the description:
"Do you need help getting rid of aches and pains? We have a wide selection of CBD products to aid in the treatment of aches and pains throughout the body, so you can go about your day stress-free."

When everything in your body hurts and getting enough sleep to keep you functioning throughout the day is foremost in your mind, *"getting rid of aches and pains"* becomes high on your priority list.

This meant that it was a no brainer for me to try the CBD, so I ordered my first 30 ml (1.01 ounce) bottle $50 CAD ($36.52 USD or £29.81) and faithfully took a dropper full every day, despite the less than pleasant taste. (Prices were correct at time of printing)

All my research, and everyone I spoke to about CBD products had the same thing to say – a sort of blanket disclaimer, to get them off the hook if you didn't receive the results their advertising was claiming. It goes something like this:

"Everyone is different with respect to how much, how long you might need to take it before you feel any results, or indeed, if you will ever receive any benefit."

In other words, while it may help some individuals, there is no guarantee that this quite expensive product will help at all. Unfortunately, after a month, I concluded that the 1,000 mg of CBD oil I had been consuming each day was doing little, if anything, to aid in the treatment of my aches and pains, and I could do without the less than pleasant taste, too. However, I convinced myself that perhaps the problem was that I just wasn't taking a high enough dosage, and I wasn't quite ready to give up on CBD, yet.

b) CBD edibles

This brought me to my next experiment with CBD edibles, and this time I chose the maximum strength hemp infused gummy bears at $110 CAD ($80.35 USD or £65.59) and faithfully chewed these for the next month. Sadly, I must report that while they certainly were tasty and I may have experienced an improvement in my mood, I didn't feel any noticeable pain relief. (Prices were correct at time of printing)

c) CB2 wellness

Next, finally my scouring of the Internet brought me to something called CB2 Wellness, from a Canadian company called *"Cannanda,"* which turned out to be what I now call *"my miracle potion."*

CANNANDA

CB2

What is CB2? Simply stated, the CB2 product is a physician formulated, small, but mighty, 5 ml (0.15 ounce) bottle containing approximately 130 drops (light oil consistency) of 100% pure and natural, terpenes derived from botanical sources.

CB2 Wellness is a powerful *"Phytocannabinoid"* formula that promises to be:

"Helpful for pain, depression, anxiety and stress, inflammation, arthritis, migraines, immune function, nausea, neurological and brain function, overall health. CB2 can also be used topically for certain skin conditions, insect bites and insect bites."

What is a phytocannabinoid? News Medical Life Sciences tell us that phytocannabinoids are: *"Cannabinoids that naturally occur in the cannabis plant and directly interact with your body's EndoCannabinoid System (ECS)."*

The endocannabinoid system is a complex signaling network of receptors within the body (CB1, CB2). The prefix *"phyto"* simply indicates that the product is derived from a plant source.

The National Library of Medicine defines phytocannabinoids as: *"Any plant derived natural product capable of either directly interacting with cannabinoid receptors or sharing chemical similarity with cannabinoids or both."*

How could I resist trying out a product that promised so much pain relief in so many areas? Of course, the answer is that I could not, and immediately ordered my first bottle.

"CB2 WELLNESS: EXTRA STRENGTH - Concentrated CB2 Oil [$31 CAD, $22.64 USD or £18.48] – The description of this CB2 product states that it helps with inflammation, pain, stress, anxiety, feeling relaxed and calm, sleep enhancing, mood balancing. (Prices were correct at time of printing)

I was so excited to receive my first bottle of CB2 and when it arrived, I was anxious to see if this product would alleviate the particularly nasty pain I was feeling in my hips every time I had to walk up the stairs.

I carefully followed the instructions for dosage. I placed 3 drops in the palm of my hand, rubbed my palms together, and held my palms over my nose to breath in the relaxing, wonderful scent for about a minute.

Soon after I heard the buzzer going off upstairs to let me know that the laundry was ready for the tumble drier, so I steeled myself for the pain I knew was coming when I walked up the stairs.

To my great astonishment and relief, the pain I had felt in my hips only shortly before was gone. Gone! **You cannot imagine how elated I was!** Now I carry this tiny bottle of CB2 Wellness everywhere with me and if I have a moment of pain all it takes is a minute to inhale those relaxing terpenes and I'm ready to go.

While of course I cannot guarantee that this product will work as well for you as it does for me (now I sound like those companies selling CBD), I can tell you from personal experience that it also works for dogs in pain (1 drop for every 25 pounds or 11.33 kgs).

This product worked so well for me that I also decided to purchase their terpene infused CB2 Hemp Seed Oil soft gels product and their CB2 Salve for targeted local relief, which also works well when rubbed into sore muscles. Always take to your health care provider before trying anything new.

d) CB2 wellness soft gels

You may be asking: *"Why buy the soft gels when the CB2 Wellness works so well?"* Simple. Anyone who has ever suffered from fibromyalgia knows that some days you feel pretty good, then it strikes back again and lays you low. You can never have enough help in your arsenal against pain, especially when it's a plant-based alternative.

I could easily see the benefits of working both the outside and inside of my body with these amazing phytocannabinoids formulas when I read on the description that: *"This oil, which is world-famous, helps to produce your body's own healing endocannabinoids (naturally occurring neurotransmitters). People use this gel for sleep issues, anxiety and pain but the benefits could extend to what YOUR body needs as this product follows your body's lead."*

"CB2 HEMP OIL CAPSULES [ORGANIC] [$39. CAD, $28.50 USD, or £23.25] – The description states: "*These are extra strength for Inflammation, Stress and Anxiety.*" (Prices were correct at time of printing)

e) CB2 Salve

Then I added the Salve for $25 CAD, ($18.30 USD or £14.90) to my arsenal and today any time I have a sore muscle, bug bite, sunburn, etc., this wonderful smelling Salve is my go-to product. (Prices were correct at time of printing)

I was more than happy to add the benefits of this salve to my routine so that I could feel what it says on the product description: *"Feel the fast-acting benefits. Targets local pain relief for soreness and muscle strains"*.

I feel truly blessed to have found the above CB2 products and hope that they work as well for you as they did for me.

f) Where to buy CB2 products
On https://cannanda.com there is a link "Where to buy" where you will see a store locator and links to buy online in Australia, UK, EU and International. I think the list of countries where to buy will expand soon.

5. Paraphernalia

The following is an overview of the more expensive paraphernalia or devices that I bought to help me in my quest for pain relief.

"Three routes to healing:
1. You must let the pain visit.
2. You must allow it to teach you.
3. You must not allow it to overstay."
~ Ijeoma Umebinyuo ~

a) Neck stretcher
While there are many neck stretching devices that cost much less, I chose to purchase the *"Liipoo Heated Neck Stretcher"* [$57 CAD, $41.70 USD, or £33.99]. Available on Amazon. (Prices were correct at time of printing)

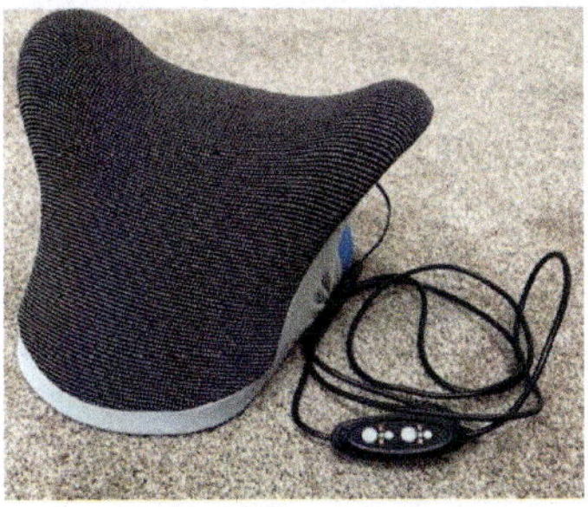

I was experiencing so much pain in my neck that I could barely turn right or left more than a few degrees and could not wait to receive this stretcher that promised much relief.

I am very happy to report that this neck stretcher provided great relief from my neck pain, even after just one 20 minutes session. At first, it feels quite uncomfortable, but then the heat (the low level is quite warm enough for me) is soothing to help you relax into it.

Now, even though I no longer suffer from neck pain, I continue to use this neck stretcher once a week to ensure relief from any tightness. This is even more important in today's high-tech world that has so many of us round shouldered and in a head forward position on our smart phones.

b) Red light belt

After much research that indicated the best red light therapy would be a device that produced both 650nm Infrared (IR) and 850nm Near Infrared (NIR), I purchased this portable red light device because it was large enough to use on any body part and because it was easy to take everywhere with me.

"Naviocean Red Light for Body Belt Device 850mm" [$110 CAD, $80.40 USD, or £65.60]. Available on Amazon. (Prices were correct at time of printing)

All I needed to read to get me interested and convinced that this was a product that I needed to add to my self-help arsenal were the words: *"speed healing"* and *"no side effects"* on Amazon reviews.

Even though this product is described as a *"Body Belt Device"* I never used it as a belt. Rather, since it is quite large, I found that it was very effective when used as a flat pad all over my body. I would begin by laying it on my legs for ten minutes (toes and feet included), and slowly work my way up my body, continuing with 10- minute increments, and then start over again at the feet, working my way up the back of the legs and again up the entire body.

After that, if I wasn't already totally relaxed and hadn't fallen asleep, I would lay it first on my right hand and forearm, followed by my upper arm and shoulder, and then the same on the left arm.

I found that this red-light device was blessedly effective in greatly diminishing my body pains, wherever they were occurring. Today, anytime I feel a twinge, or have a sore muscle, this belt soon relieves the symptoms.

c) Cold laser

I then decided to try a cold laser device. [$260 CAD, $190 USD, or £155.05]. Available on Amazon. (Prices were correct at time of printing)

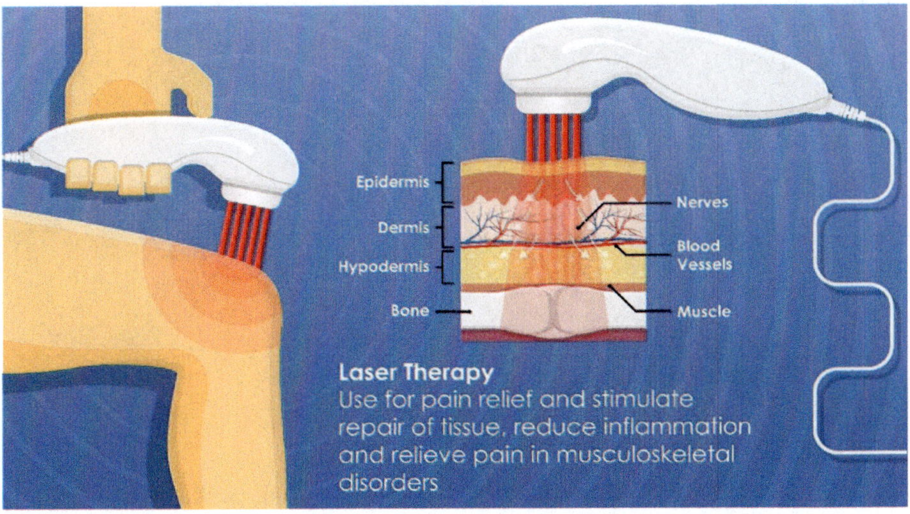

Having carried out extensive research about cold laser therapy for pain, I was convinced this device needed to be added to my *"pain arsenal"*.

The portability and easy recharging of this product was ideal for me. This device is light weight and easy to hold and I found it to be very effective for relieving pain in smaller, specific areas of my body, such as a knee, shoulder or wrist.

This was a valuable tool in my quest for reducing fibro pain and will continue to be helpful for myself when I've had a particularly busy day, and indeed for helping any of my pups with muscle or arthritis pain.

As it is so easy to use and efficient, there is sometimes a bit of competition with respect to who is first up to use it, as my husband has realized how effective this tool is for him.

d) Standing desk

Then I purchased a standing desk converter [$150 CAD, $109.60 USD, or £89.45]. It is foldable and has different height levels. Available on Amazon. (Prices were correct at time of printing). This is my standing desk converter:

I know what you're thinking. What does a standing desk have to do with fibromyalgia paraphernalia? As mentioned before: *"Sitting is the new smoking"*. It is well known that a sedentary lifestyle leads to many serious health issues.

I helped to create my fibro condition by choosing to be a work-at-home workaholic focussing on my writing (to the distraction of all else), sitting behind a computer screen for many long hours each day, without breaks.

Thankfully I have (better late than never) learned my painful lesson, and while I am still sitting behind a computer screen a lot, I now have a standing desk. I am no longer sitting for hours at a time, and instead can sit for an hour, raise the desk and stand for approx. 30 minutes whilst doing some gentle moves and stretches.

Standing whilst working somehow makes it easier to take a short break, walk away from the computer, do maybe 20 minutes of meditation, or perhaps a short nap and then return refreshed.

According to Harvard Health, the health benefits of using a standing desk are not to be ignored. It is known that sitting all day, besides being terrible for your muscles, nerves and circulation, is linked to a higher risk of suffering from several very concerning health issues, including:

- Anxiety and depression
- Back problems – fascia gets sticky!
- Cancer
- Deep vein thrombosis
- Diabetes
- Gaining weight
- Heart disease

- High blood pressure
- High cholesterol
- Hip problems – fascia gets sticky!
- Neck problems– fascia gets sticky!
- Obesity
- Premature death
- Stroke
- Varicose veins
- Weak glutes and leg muscles– fascia gets sticky!

A study carried out by the American Cancer Society reveals: *"Women and men who both sat more and were less physical were 94% and 48% more likely, respectively, to die compared with those who reported sitting the least and being most active."*

That's a very scary statistic that anyone concerned about improving their health needs to take seriously. I'm sure you'll agree that the benefits associated with changing over to a standing desk are well worth considering when they include:

- Better circulation
- Improved mood
- Improved muscle tone
- Improved posture
- Increased activity
- Increased energy
- Increased lifespan
- Less neck and back pain
- Less risk for all the problems listed under "very concerning health issues"
- Lower blood sugar and cholesterol

It will take a while to get used to a standing desk, and you may begin to feel pains in different places (especially your feet), so start slowly and set a goal to work your way up to standing 5 to 15 minutes out of every hour.

e) Zero gravity chair

You may not be familiar with a zero-gravity (ZG) chair because there are many chairs sold under this name that are not truly zero gravity. Please be aware that if you type the words *"zero gravity chair"* into a search browser, the results will often show you chairs that are not ZG.

As a rule of thumb, when considering the purchase of a ZG chair: if it is listed as a poolside lounger, garden furniture or patio chair that partially reclines, it most likely is NOT a zero-gravity chair. With a true *"zero-*

gravity" chair, when in the fully reclined position, your feet will be above your heart.

Gravity will no longer push down on your body and you will feel weightless, like an astronaut in space, hence the word zero-gravity. Without gravity, there is space between your discs, and your weight is evenly distributed allowing muscles, ligaments and tendons to completely relax in a way that no other chair could ever accomplish.

A partially reclined chair can be quite comfortable but to really experience the full benefits of a truly ZG chair, so that you can completely unwind and relax, it needs to recline far enough to allow your feet to be above your heart.

The health benefits associated with a true ZG chair include:

- Improved blood flow
- Improved breathing
- Improved digestion
- Improved energy
- Joint pressure relief
- Muscle pressure relief
- Pain relief
- Relief from swollen ankles, legs
- Spinal pressure relief
- Tension relief

I was lucky enough to have already owned one of these chairs for quite a few years prior to fibromyalgia and once I reconnected with how much better this chair made me feel, I made sure that I took advantage of my personal *"decompression chamber"* every day.

Sitting for a few minutes, half an hour, or longer in a chair that is truly ZG is a holiday from anything that hurts. In fact, my personal experience was (and still is) that within minutes of reclining I would be so relaxed that I would fast asleep.

Some ZG chairs also have heat and massage functions, and while you can easily pay many thousand dollars for a true ZG chair, depending on style, construction materials, features (heat, massage), and whether it's operated manually or electrically, you can also find one that is easier on the wallet.

Currently the average price range for these types of **true** ZG chairs ranges between $2,000 CAD, $1,461.60 USD, or £1,600 and $8,000 CAD, $5,846.50 USD, or £6,398. (Prices were correct at time of printing)

At the very minimum, when looking for a true ZG chair, besides making sure it really is a true ZG chair, and deciding whether you want massage, heat, or a manual or powered recline, there are several other considerations to be aware of:

- Adjustable head and footrest
- Easy to recline
- Good cushioning
- Long-lasting materials
- Lumbar pillow
- Strong base
- Support for the arms

I highly recommend that you defy gravity if you can afford it. Even if you're not suffering from fibro pain, the fully reclined position of this chair is unique in its ability to completely neutralize the affects gravity is having on your body to allow healing, repair, and even prevent aging.

Hammock

A hammock is a much cheaper solution and can also give you a very relaxing position to lie in, to help with your pains but make sure your feet are placed above your heart for maximum effect. There are many indoor and outdoor hammocks available on Amazon.

You can also buy "Antigravity hammocks". These hang down from the ceiling.

I hope that outlining what pills, potions and paraphernalia I chose to personally align myself with during my journey with fibromyalgia will also be helpful to you. I would also encourage you to carry out your own research because it is highly likely that there are many more very helpful products out there that can be beneficial in your quest to shorten your recovery time.

"Wake up – Kick Ass – Repeat"

Chapter 10: Find *Your* Mantra

Finding a mantra that works for you will help you in your journey to eliminate fibromyalgia from your life because when you are in pain, words that make you feel powerful help to reduce pain and give you determination to succeed.

A mantra is simply a syllable, word or group of words or sounds that is an *"instrument of the mind."* When you break down the word itself into syllables, *"man"* is referring to your mind, while *"tra"* means transport.

The word *"mantra"* (from the Sanskrit language) originally meant a primordial *"sacred sound"* that was chanted during a wide variety of religious and spiritual practices with the goal being to transform mind, body and spirit. While the mantra I am referring to in this section is more correctly termed an *"affirmation"* the goal remains the same.

"The question isn't who is going to let me,
the question is who is going to stop me?"
~ Ayn Rand ~

During meditation, the repeated words or sounds of a mantra can be anything. Repeating a mantra out loud (or to yourself) is more about transcending the exterior noise and jumbled activity of the brain rather than the particular sounds so that you can focus on the moment.

However, the words of a mantra can also certainly have personal meaning for you, especially if they make you feel powerfully in charge of your life, help to keep you on a positive path and add a needed boost of determination to your plan to get rid of fibromyalgia in your life.

I personally connect with the words *"Wake up – Kick Ass – Repeat"* because saying them helps to set your intention and get you into a determined, confident mindset at the beginning of your day so that you will be ready to do what's necessary to win the fibro battle.

Find your own affirmation phrase because it doesn't matter what it is, so long as saying the words out loud or to yourself evokes a powerful feeling of confidence that you can carry with you throughout your day.

The following blank lines are for you to write down your own ideas and inspirations about what your mantra might be.

"Wake up – Kick Ass – Repeat"

Chapter 11: Find the Funny Side of Life

Fibromyalgia is painful. Laughter relieves pain. More laughter equals less pain – it's a simple, effective formula.

"Sometimes you got to specifically go out of your way to get into trouble. It's called fun."
~ Robin Williams ~

However, for those who suffer from daily pain, and may have been choosing to keep to themselves, or are living on a deserted island with only coconuts to converse with, finding the funny side of life and connecting with what makes you happy may be a bit of a challenge.

OK, you know that humor is beneficial to your life because it reduces pain, which makes you happier, and makes you healthier because it's easier to cope with stress when you have less pain.

However, when you learn how to take a new perspective on an old situation and learn how to laugh at yourself and especially at life in general, you are literally protecting yourself from the ravages of negative emotions (anger, anxiety, depression).

Laughter is directly related to longevity. Yes, more laughter equals longer life. So, rather than letting every little thing irritate and get under your skin, how do you learn to find and stay on the funny side of life?

"I felt so bad last night for having this one-night stand, the next day I got another one for the other side of the bed."
~ Unknown ~

Sometimes what's necessary in finding the funny side of life involves learning how to see normal daily occurrences in a different light or simply finding ways to look at things that might otherwise upset you in a way that brings a smile instead of a frown.

There are many life situations that have *"stages"* or *"steps"* routinely assigned to them that you may be familiar with such as the 5 Stages of Addiction Recovery, the 12 Step AA Program, and the 5 States of Grief, but did you know that there are 4 stages assigned to finding the funny?

You might be wondering why funny only gets 4 stages. All that really matters is that the steps or stages are there merely as a starting point or guideline to help get you moving in a successful (funny) direction. You can learn how to turn painful situations into something you can laugh about.

Step 1: It is a gift

Decide that everything that occurs in your life is a gift or an opportunity to grow and make your life better. This gift, whether it be fibromyalgia pains or something else you have previously found upsetting, when looked upon as a gift, offers you a valuable way to learn more about yourself, and make better decisions.

When the gift is physical fibro pain, and you learn to find humor in it, you are on your way toward breaking the cycle, turning pain into healing and becoming much more joyful about every little thing life may throw at you. Say thank you!

Step 2: Accept it

When you take a moment to acknowledge and accept how you feel, both physically and emotionally, you remove much of the power it holds over you, rather than allowing it to dictate a negative mood for the rest of your day.

Step 3: Improve it

Take action to make the pain better because resting in your pain and feeling sorry for yourself is not going to improve anything. Maybe this means reducing your pain by screaming your favorite swear words into a pillow, or maybe it means taking a 5-minute breath break. There are so many simple ways to take action and improve it.

Step 4: Choose it

You are much more powerful than you may realize. Why? Simply because only you are in control of your thoughts and how you choose to react to each situation, and only you always have the power of choice.

You can choose to throw a fit of anger or grind your teeth in frustration every time you feel a new fibro pain, or you can choose to laugh and say to yourself, *"That's an interesting sensation"* and then follow steps 1, 2 and 3 above. It's up to you to choose to languish in your misery or laugh and feel better.

Honestly, most of us take ourselves far too seriously. The good news is that once you begin to see the funny side of everyday occurrences, they will begin to present themselves more and more often, until pretty much anything that happens can make you laugh.

Perhaps the stressed-out driver behind you is expressing his toxic day by leaning on his horn at every opportunity because he created his own frustrating scene by not leaving home soon enough time to get to work on time. Rather than allowing his self-anger to invade your happy thoughts, think about those cartoons you used to watch as a child.

I don't know what cartoons made you laugh when you were a child. Whenever I'm in a traffic situation and I hear someone needlessly honking their horn, I smile and recall one of my favorite childhood cartoons.

I imagine that driver to be Wiley Coyote trying to catch the Roadrunner by strapping himself to a live rocket with a short fuse that soon blows up in his face. The Roadrunner always smiles and goes on his way. It makes me laugh, and I also feel a bit sorry for the stressed-out horn honker.

What do you call a group of cars playing instruments?
[A traffic jam]

Training yourself to see the funny side of life can be your secret weapon that will easily diffuse any type of painful situation, whether psychological or physical.

Have less pain, feel happier, be healthier, and enjoy a longer life when you choose to find the funny side of life.

"Wake up – Kick Ass – Repeat"

Chapter 12: What Makes You Happy?

While it can be challenging to feel happy when you are suffering from fibromyalgia pain, finding that happy place is even more important. It's time to find, and then learn to really appreciate the little things in life that particularly make you happy because:

"No medicine cures what happiness cannot."
~ Gabriel Garcia Marquez ~

Whether it's drifting through cloud filled skies suspended from a hot air balloon, something as simple as leaning against a tall tree and listening to the breeze flutter the leaves or reading this book and finding out about all the simple, and many free steps you can take to help remove fibro from your life, it doesn't matter what it is.

What matters is that you acknowledge the little (or big) things in life that make you particularly happy, and that you then take the time to enjoy them.

All too often we get caught up in the bustling, daily routines of life and it becomes easier to continue with the familiar rather than giving yourself permission to step outside of your habitual routine and make an effort to schedule in the time to do something that truly makes you happy.

Sometimes it can be quite difficult to really know what makes you happy because this usually will change over time. What made you happy when you were a 12-year-old may be entirely different now.

As you age, you may not consciously consider what genuinely makes you happy because you are being too busy getting on with the day-to-day experiences of life. However, no matter your age, it is very important to make the time to engage in activities that make you happy, especially if you've been spending your life chasing what you think will make you happy in the future (the big house, the fancy car, the top of the corporate ladder).

When you get caught up too much in thinking about future happiness, you often forget to take the time to discover what makes you happy **in the here and now.**

While you're thinking about what makes you happy in your life today, here's a few points that outline why personal happiness is so important, which may help you to discover what your happiness pattern may be. Doing things that make you happy is important because:

- It can help you to be more productive in your life
- It helps to improve relationships with others
- It helps you to believe in yourself
- It helps you to grow and learn new things
- It helps you to stay motivated
- It improves your health
- It results in less negative and pain messages to your brain

When you're really thinking about what makes you happy, forget about being materialistic, or projecting happiness into the future. Instead, focus on the little things in your day that you take the time to enjoy because these are all moments of happiness.

Consider that sitting still to watch a hummingbird at a feeder, taking a walk through brightly colored autumn leaves, enjoying a freshly brewed cup of coffee or star gazing on a quiet summer evening are all moments of happiness.

Of course, while your happiness may involve a large financial commitment, if you want to take a year off work and travel the world, once you begin to think about the daily things that make you happy, you will soon see a pattern emerge and realize that these things need not be costly or involve long periods of time.

I will end this chapter with a quote from an American lawyer, politician, statesman and 16th President of the United States, who very succinctly summed up happiness when he said,

"Most folks are about as happy as they make up their minds to be."
~ Abraham Lincoln ~

The following writing lines are for you to write down all the things that make you happy. Don't just write them down but also practice happy things in everyday life.

"Wake up – Kick Ass – Repeat"

Chapter 13: Therapy Treatments

There are many therapy treatments out there recommended for helping to relieve fibromyalgia pain, some of which take a more traditional straight line, while others are more fluid and circuitous.

This chapter is all about encouraging you to try various healing therapies, because as Dr. Seuss said:

"The more that you read, the more things you will know. The more that you learn, the more places you'll go."

My search for relief from debilitating pain sent me down a path that included the following therapy modalities that helped me. Have an open mind and discover what works best for you. We are all different: a therapy that worked for me might not work for you and vice versa.

1. Yoga Therapy

The Harvard Medical School has interesting things to say about using yoga to reduce pain:

"Yoga is a mind-body and exercise practice that combines breath control, meditation, and movements to stretch and strengthen muscles. What sets yoga apart from most other exercise programs is that it places as great an emphasis on mental fitness as on physical fitness.

People have been doing yoga for thousands of years. Given its history, several types of yoga have developed. The most popular form practiced in the United States is hatha yoga — of which there are numerous variations.

*Yoga can help people with arthritis, **fibromyalgia**, migraine, low back pain, and many other types of chronic pain conditions. A study published in Annals of Internal Medicine found that among 313 people with chronic low back pain, a weekly yoga class increased mobility more than standard medical care for the condition. Another study published at nearly the same time found that yoga was comparable to standard exercise therapy in relieving chronic low back pain.*

A meta-analysis of 17 studies that included more than 1,600 participants concluded that yoga could improve daily function among *people with **fibromyalgia** osteoporosis-related curvature of the spine. Practicing yoga also improved mood and psychosocial well-being."*

2. Qigong and Tai Chi

Every Day Health has the following to say about these 2 gentle, repeated movement exercise therapies:

"Qigong (pronounced "chee-gong") and tai chi are ancient Chinese practices that involve meditation, controlled breathing, and movement to improve a person's mental and physical health. According to the National Center for Complementary and Integrative Health (NCCIH), these techniques offer various wellness benefits, including reducing chronic pain.

*When researchers followed 226 people with **fibromyalgia** (a disorder characterized by widespread musculoskeletal pain) for one year, they found that after 24 weeks, participants who practiced tai chi once or twice a week reported more improvement in their symptom control than those who performed aerobic exercises twice a week. And the longer they practiced tai chi, the better the results.*

*Authors of the study concluded "Tai chi mind-body treatment results in similar or greater improvement in symptoms than aerobic exercise, the current most commonly prescribed nondrug treatment, for a variety of outcomes for patients with **fibromyalgia**."*

3. Massage Therapy

Most people are aware of the general benefits associated with massage therapy. However, you may be one of those who thinks that massage is something that the idle rich indulge in to relax, after a tiring day on the golf course, at one of those fancy spas in an elite hotel.

If this sounds like you, perhaps it's time to think a little differently about using massage as a way toward less pain and improved health, because although perhaps out of the price range for too many, massage is a valuable tool in your search for a healthier and happier you, especially deep tissue massage.

A very long list of maladies can greatly benefit from massage therapy. Massage is not just for those who spend their days looking for ways to indulge themselves because it's not just fibro sufferers who can benefit. Massage therapy is known to improve:

- Anxiety
- Depression
- Digestive Disorders

- Fibromyalgia
- Headache
- Insomnia
- Nerve Pain
- Post-operative Care
- Scar Tissue
- Soft Tissue Sprains and Injuries
- Sports Injuries
- Temporomandibular Disorders

While the above list includes fibromyalgia as a stand-alone condition, at least 6 are part of the plethora of conditions that many fibromyalgia sufferers (including myself) have experienced. Deep muscle massage has really helped me in my quest to beat the fibro blues.

As an example, I would begin my massage with many painful complaints, and then after an hour, walk out with much greater ease, far less pain and a smile on my face.

The heavier pressure of deep muscle massage is much more effective for relieving fibromyalgia pain than a gentle Swedish type of massage because it helps to relieve tension in deeper connective tissues and muscles that are often the source of chronic pain.

When you're suffering from fibro pain, whenever you can afford to, I would highly recommend that you consider a deep muscle massage because it is my personal experience that massage therapy really does help.

4. Counselling Therapy

While counselling might not be foremost in your mind to help relieve your chronic pain, if you are open to it, a psychologist can certainly help you in many ways.

"The unexamined life is not worth living."
~ Socrates ~

I have mentioned it before but certainly worth repeating here as it is crucially important:

You cannot physically heal completely if your mind is troubled and not calm and happy. Negative emotions can lock up your body if you don't process them: anger, guilt fear, worry.

Therapy is a great way to learn new coping skills and relaxation techniques, change belief patterns that are getting in the way of healing, get closer to understanding the root cause of your pain, and set yourself on a path to learning how to help empower yourself while also addressing anxiety or depression.

A psychologist can support and help make suggestions about possible lifestyle changes and other therapies that may be just what you need to distract yourself and break the cycle of chronic pain so that you can connect with the power of your own body and focus on a positive path toward curing yourself.

Having an honest conversation with a professional sympathetic ear about how fibro is affecting your life and who can offer advice while you learn how to manage your emotions and stress level can go a long way toward helping to reduce the intensity of your pain.

I tend toward being the self-help, do the research, read the books, figure it out for yourself sort of person. However, when I was in the midst of my own fibro battleground, I found that talking with a counsellor was extremely helpful.

It was important for me to hear from an unbiased third party that being a workaholic, never taking a holiday, a weekend off, or engaging in any activity beyond work, was beyond unhealthy and definitely not the way forward. In other words, I needed to learn an entirely new lifestyle, and while doing so also let go of feeling guilty about it, if I was going to have any hope of curing what had become my life of chronic pain.

Counselling therapy could be a valuable first step toward discovering what you need to work on, and then focusing on a plan that will see you safely back to your own happy, pain free self. A counsellor can find your weaknesses and I believe that the weaknesses we attempt to bottle up in our character can become our strengths.

People with greater social support (whether family members, friends or professionals) experience less anxiety and depression and in the long run are more resilient, able to take control and better manage their own health.

When dealing with chronic pain it's important to know your limit, make a plan to work within it, and always ask for help when you need it.

5. Sensory Deprivation Therapy - Floating

Sensory deprivation (also known as perceptual isolation) is the *"deliberate reduction or removal of stimuli from one or more of the senses."*
While there are many different mediums that could be referred to as sensory deprivation, I'm talking about a dark, soundproof flotation tank filled with about 12 inches (30.48 cm) of skin temperature water and approximately 1500 pounds (680.38 kgs) of magnesium rich, dissolved Epsom salt.

The idea behind the float tank is that when inside, you are cut off from all outside stimuli so that you can experience nothing. There is nothing to disturb your peace but the beating of your own heart while you assume a relaxing position and float weightlessly.

It is believed that the physical and psychological benefits associated with floating weightlessly, in complete silence and darkness, include improvement of stress, anxiety and chronic pain, all of which are known to be present when you are suffering from the effects of fibromyalgia.

Floating weightlessly is good for your health and helps many people achieve pain free bliss. The high concentration of magnesium in the Epsom salt is very beneficial for your health.

Magnesium is the second most ample element in your body. Many are suffering from magnesium deficiency, which is vital to maintaining health and general well-being. This means that the health benefits associated with saltwater floating, are many:

- **Bone health:** magnesium is essential for helping calcium to be assimilated into your bones to make them stronger.
- **Detoxification**: when toxins and heavy metals are flushed from your cells, besides clearing out harmful substances you don't want in your body, this will help to ease muscle pain.
- **Diabetes prevention**: magnesium helps to improve insulin sensitivity and aids blood glucose control, which can prevent or reduce severity.

- **Heart health**: magnesium improves the health of the circulatory system and heart by lowering blood pressure and helping to prevent blood clots and hardening of the arteries.
- **Migraine relief**: magnesium can help to ease or prevent migraine headaches.
- **Mood improvement**: because magnesium helps bind serotonin (the happy hormone) your mood will improve, and you will enjoy better sleep.
- **Relaxation**: magnesium helps to elevate your brain chemicals to create a feeling of relaxation and well-being.
- **Stress relief**: magnesium is a natural stress-reliever. When you're stressed, which is almost always the case when suffering from the chronic pain with fibromyalgia, the excess adrenaline drains magnesium from your system.

Experiencing nothing for a whole 75 minutes sounded like a blissful mini holiday for this workaholic personality. I was really excited about trying this.

I followed the instructions posted at the floating facility I attended, arrived 15 minutes early for my first float so that I could learn how everything worked, and was left to my own private float room. After showering, I entered the tank and relaxed into a floating position, which was easy to do because the water was super buoyant, so much so that I almost felt like I was wearing several lifejackets.

While I could choose to listen to relaxing music, leave the soft, colored lights on, or be in complete silence, I chose to be in silent darkness, turned the lights off and closed the lid. In total darkness and complete silence, I could hear my own heart beating. As directed, I took slow deep breaths and could hear my heart rate beginning to slow. Then something totally unexpected occurred.

After approximately 10 minutes floating, I began to feel uncomfortably hot, so I opened the lid a few inches to let some air in. Unfortunately, this did not help me feel any better and my stomach was starting to feel quite unsettled, so I moved to the handle end of the flotation tank and opened the lid completely.

I sat upright and calmly sat there for about 5 more minutes, hoping to feel better. Nothing improved, so I got myself out and took a cold shower. Now my stomach is really starting to churn and I'm feeling like I may throw up, so I quickly got dressed and exited my private room to the relief of the cooler air outside. I had a few sips of water and sat on the bench hoping that my stomach would settle, while I called my husband to come and pick me up.

I thought I might throw up on the ride home but managed to make it home just in time to run through the door and throw up in the bathroom. It was about 4 hours later until I began to feel better. I suspect that perhaps this unfortunate outcome was the result of me being one of those individuals that runs very hot, and the float room was for me, uncomfortably humid.

While this type of floatation therapy is a great help to many, even though it turned out not to be the best of experiences for me, it was still a valuable lesson to me that not every therapy is going to be a positive experience for everyone. In other words, you need to do your own research, try new therapies and find the ones that work for you.

6. Hydrotherapy

This branch (or should I say pool or ocean) of alternative medicine (also called water cure, water therapy, aquatic therapy, or balneotherapy), is simply using water for pain relief. In other words, check yourself into the local recreation center that has a pool and go swimming or do gentle exercises.

When I first began to feel my fibro pains, I forgot that I had a potential treatment inside the very building where I live – a pool and a hot tub. Besides being more relaxing and easier to do with the support of the water around you, exercising in a pool can burn more calories with much less fatigue, and you can exercise longer with less pain.

Important: Be careful not to over-stretch or over-exercise in the water. Often, you don't feel the pain when you are in the water but you do a few hours later or the next day. If that happens, you have overdone it.

A study was carried out by The National Library of Medicine (Scientific Evidence-Based Effects of Hydrotherapy). This study concluded that fatigue, tension, memory and mood negative state points are decreased by winter swimming on a regular basis. There was an improved general well-being in the swimmers suffering from fibromyalgia, asthma or rheumatism.

If easy access to a lake or the ocean had been possible for me, rather than just pool therapy, I would have certainly added winter swimming to my fibro treatments.

When your day is marred by fibromyalgia pain and movement is a challenge, hydrotherapy can really help to keep you going (without adding more pain).

If you have access to some form of hydrotherapy, why wouldn't you add this to your routine, especially since the benefits are:

- Decreased anxiety
- Decreased depression
- Decreased stress
- Faster recovery from surgery
- Flushing of toxins
- Improved balance and coordination
- Improved circulation
- Improved healing
- Improved immune system
- Improved range of motion
- Pain relief
- Reduced inflammation
- Relaxed muscles
- Weight loss

Whether it's a warm water recreation center swimming pool, a cold plunge pool, detoxing at a natural mineral spa, winter swimming or a dead sea salt soak in your own bathtub, there is no doubt that many forms of hydrotherapy can go a long way toward helping to heal your fibro blues.

7. Infrared Sauna Therapy

While the traditional Finnish style hot air sauna can certainly help to improve mood, detox, and relax painful muscles, for some, the heat can be too intense to bear for longer than a few short minutes.

Rather than heating the air around you, the infrared sauna uses light to directly penetrate the skin and heat the body. This results in a more comfortable experience as the temperature is lower compared to a traditional sauna.

There have been many scientific studies outlining the countless health benefits associated with the regular use of an infrared sauna:

- Decreased inflammation
- Decreased pain
- Decreased stress
- Improved cardiovascular health
- Improved circulation
- Improved mood
- Improved recovery from muscle overuse
- Improved resistance to infection
- Increased exercise tolerance
- Increased metabolism
- Less risk of complications from diabetes
- Lowered blood pressure
- Lowered incidence of dementia
- Promotion of deep sleep
- Promotion of faster wound healing
- Promotion of nerve repair
- Reduced oxidative damage to cells
- Reduction in allergies
- Release of toxins
- Relief from joint stiffness
- Relief from muscle, joint and back pain
- Slowed skin aging
- Stronger immune system
- Weight loss

Considering all the numerous health benefits associated with infrared sauna therapy, who wouldn't want to take advantage of this type of therapy, whether or not you are suffering from fibromyalgia?

I was fortunate enough to have the opportunity to enjoy this type of therapy at a friend's home several times throughout my fibro journey, and I felt the positive effects right away. My only regret was that I did not have the space to have one permanently set up in my own home, because I am certain that daily use would have greatly increased my recovery rate.

The good news is that, compared to the traditional hot air sauna, there are now many manufacturers making it fairly easy (if you have the space), and relatively affordable (beginning around $2,000 CDN,

$1,461.60 USD, or £1,602) to set up your very own infrared sauna right in your home. (Prices were correct at time of printing)

8. Aromatherapy

While other scents in nature have the power to enhance emotional and physical health, aromatherapy refers to the practice of absorbing or inhaling the scent of aromatic essential oils (concentrated plant extracts) to help promote health and well-being.

While ancient cultures have practiced aromatherapy for thousands of years, this holistic healing practice is becoming more widely recognized in the fields of traditional medicine and science. Better late than never, I say.

Aromatherapy works when absorbed by the skin (the largest organ of your body) and/or through your sense of smell and is easily attainable in many different locations (health food stores, grocery stores, online, etc.). There are many essential oils available, each with its own unique healing properties, that when blended together with other oils synergistically provide even more benefits.

While my favorite *"go to"* essential oil scent is Lavender, according to the National Association for Holistic Aromatherapy, the most popular essential oils include:

- Clay Sage
- Cypress
- Eucalyptus
- Fennel
- Geranium
- Ginger
- Helichrysum
- Lavender
- Lemon
- Lemongrass
- Mandarin
- Neroli
- Patchouli
- Peppermint
- Roman Chamomile
- Rose
- Rosemary
- Tea Tree
- Vetiver
- Ylang Ylang

Here's an astonishing fact: it takes 250 pounds (113.39 kg) of lavender flowers to make just 1 pound (0.45 kg) of lavender essential oil! An unbelievably large number of flowers were harvested to bring you this amazing oil, hence why the price is high.

It's precisely *because* it takes so much of the plant to make a small amount of oil that makes the essential oil such a powerful botanical medicine. Some of the health benefits attributed to using essential oils in your daily routine include:

- Calms the senses
- Clears sinuses
- Fights fatigue
- Heals wounds
- Improves job performance
- Improves memory
- Improves mood
- Improves sleep
- Increases attention
- Kills bacteria, viruses and fungus
- Lowers blood pressure
- Promotes hair growth
- Reduces inflammation
- Reduces joint pain
- Relieves anxiety and stress
- Relieves depression
- Relieves headaches and nausea
- Relieves pain
- Supports digestion

Be mindful when choosing to use essential oils because some are known to cause harm when used in excess, and there might be some you are allergic to. Keep in mind that in their concentrated form, they are very strong. Use only a few drops. It's best to dilute them with water or with a carrier oil to apply to the skin.

Another great way to benefit from the use of essential oils while making your entire home smell wonderful is to put a few drops in a diffuser. When mixed with water so that the tiny molecules are dispersed into the air where you can breathe them in, the aroma will stimulate your central nervous system to quickly elicit a reduction in feelings of anxiety or stress. No matter how you may decide to add the benefits of essential oil aromatherapy to your healing routine, read up, test it first (perhaps on a tiny bit of skin) to make sure you are not allergic. Use sparingly, purchase organic, high quality and choose the oils that will be most helpful for your situation.

"If you believe in aromatherapy... it works!... If you don't believe in aromatherapy... it works!"
~ Christina Proano-Carrion ~

9. Scalar Wave Therapy

I can hear you say: "*What on earth is Scalar Wave Therapy?*" Most people don't know what it is and neither did I pre-fibro. In my personal experience scalar wave is ***the* best therapy of all**. Did I save the best for last? Yes, I did. If you can afford it, I strongly advice you do a few sessions.

"What some folks call impossible is just stuff they haven't seen before."
~ Robin Williams ~

While it can be a challenge to accurately describe what scalar wave therapy is, I will do my best not to confuse you with too much scientific mumbo jumbo, because you just need to know that it works.

To put it **very** simply: you lie down (or sit) on a comfortable chair, surrounded by computer screens in the room. Usually there are other people in the room with you.

Although you may have never heard about it before reading this book, scalar wave has been in use as an effective healing therapy for over 2 decades. The multiple health benefits attributed to this Energy Enhancement System (EESystem) is finally being discovered by those outside the unconventional health treatment arena.

This amazing technology, developed over 20 years ago by Dr. Sandra Rose Michael (Ph.D, DNM, DCSJl), uses custom-installed computers to generate morphogenic energy fields that have the power to promote healing.

What is a *"morphogenic energy field"* and how does this relate to your health? This is a deeply scientific question that is not easily answered for those without a scientific background. I will give it my best shot, as I understand it, in the simplest of terms.

A morphogenic energy field is the boundary of the energy field created by your nervous system's electromagnetic field. Some healing arts and various cultures refer to the morphogenic energy field as your *"Life Force,"* your *"Chi,"* your "*Chakras*" or your *"Aura,"* and believe that if this is unbalanced, you will have a challenged nervous system.

Enter the EESystem which, although few mainstream individuals or more traditional healing organizations have knowledge of it, has been recognized at countless conferences around the world, including medical, scientific and professional.

Every life form, whether it be human, animal or vegetable is made of unimaginably tiny atoms that we cannot see. Each human cell (of which there are tens of trillions) contains 100 trillion atoms that are made up of electrons, neutrons and protons and it's the flow of electrons within the atoms that create the energy that gives us life.

This internal electrical current running through your body is an important language of communication that your cells and organs rely upon. To keep your body functioning at an optimum energy level, cellular communication is critical for all your bodily functions. While there's plenty of science behind scalar wave therapy, suffice it to say that the status of your health begins with the electrical charge within your cells.

Simply stated, you will experience health and a feeling of wellness when there is a high electrical charge within your cells. On the opposite side, as I'm sure you can imagine, when your cells are partially drained or maintaining a low electrical charge, you will experience tiredness, disease, chronic pain and a less than healthy body.

As they say, because a picture is worth a thousand words, I offer the following example of cellular charge in your cells, and what happens when the charge becomes too low:

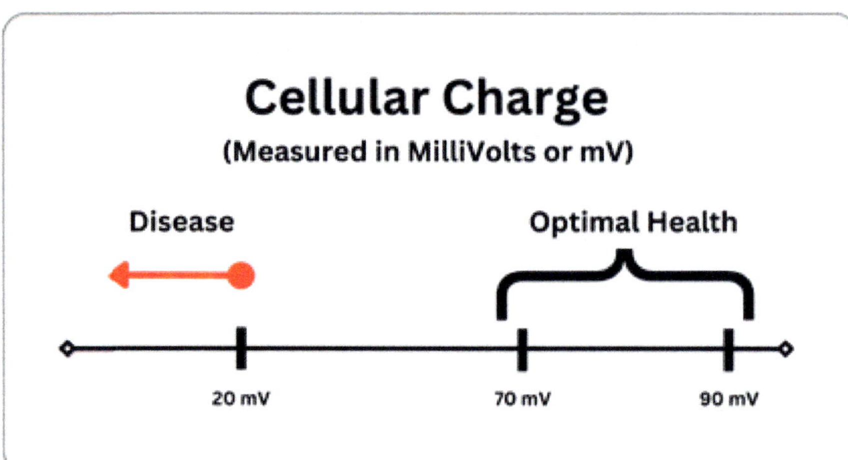

As you can see from the above diagram, healthy cells in your body will operate at a charge of between 70 and 90 mV (MilliVolts). When the charge level decreases to below 20 mV, aging and disease begins to set in. An easy, powerful and very relaxing way to reverse a decreased charge level within your cells is to enter a scalar wave field. Being in the presence of a scalar wave field will excite your personal electromagnetic field which in turn will help to return your cells to an optimal charge level.

"The treatments themselves do not 'cure" the condition, they simply restore the body's self-healing ability."
~ Leon Chaitow ~

Think of it like hooking a depleted electric vehicle into a live electric wall socket. If you do this for long enough, the cells in the vehicle's batteries will charge up to maximum capacity so the vehicle can once again be fully operational. Once your cells are operating at a higher charge, cellular regeneration is possible and the body literally now has the power to heal itself by releasing trapped toxins, lengthening telomeres (turning back the aging clock) and even repairing damage in your DNA structure.

When you give your body what it needs, you then have within your grasp the power to heal yourself of virtually anything. Generally, what needs the most *"repair"* attention in your body will be addressed first, and then on down to smaller repairs.

I don't know about you, but all the above was certainly something I wanted for my future health, and thankfully, when I was moving forward with winning my fibro battle, I was fortunate enough to live in an area where I had access to a Wellness Centre that had recently installed an EESystem.

My first 2-hour session with the EESystem ($150 CAD, $109.60 USD, or £89.45) was one of the most relaxing 2 hours I've ever spent.

There were several other individuals in the quiet, darkened room, reclining in semi-zero gravity chairs, with cozy blankets, and almost everyone was soon asleep. 2 hours passed very quickly, and I found myself feeling happy, relaxed and almost pain free as I was leaving the facility. To say I was hooked was a very big understatement because I could not wait to return for my next session.

Just 2 days later, I returned for my next 2-hour EES session. While this time was equally as relaxing as the first, and my aches and pains were markedly improved, I noted that my feelings of elation were not quite as pronounced as they were after my first session. Most likely because the mV charge in my cells had already increased. I also felt quite tired, which is apparently a normal after effect, and later in the day I enjoyed a blissfully peaceful nap.

After my third EES session, I was beginning to feel like myself again, and before I knew it, I was easily getting up from a sitting position, walking up and down stairs without my usual *"Ow!"* and enjoying a much more restful sleep, with a greatly improved mood and no drug intervention whatsoever.

I was so elated to have found what for me personally **was the holy grail of pain relief**, and even though these sessions were quite pricey for the average person, while also keeping up with my other therapies, I was determined to continue to enjoy the benefits of scalar wave therapy whenever I could afford to (or whenever they had a sale).

I know you're now thinking, *"How many sessions do you need to get your cells charged to the optimum (70 to 90mV level)?"* Short answer: As many as it takes because this would depend upon your current age, how much you may have abused your health over time, and how much healing your body may need. However, you might need up to 20 hours. You are a unique individual, that has chosen your individual lifestyle, which has resulted in your own individual aches and pains.

All this means is that how many scalar wave sessions you may need to get your cell's mV charges boosted to an optimum level, and how long it may take to heal you of your ailments could be vastly different from my own. I wish there was a way to check the mV charge in your own cells, because then you would know precisely when you might need to return for another EES session. In any event, while today I have eliminated the so-called *"incurable*" fibromyalgia scourge, and am now pain free, I continue to get my cells topped up every so often just as a preventative measure.

10. Other Therapies to Consider

There are just so many new and interesting, non-invasive, alternative medicine therapy modalities for relieving pain and improving health to choose from these days. From the therapies listed below, I have personally found acupuncture to be highly effective for past health issues and I tried Reiki once but fell asleep during the session.

While I did not use any of these therapies when I was curing myself from fibromyalgia, I have no doubt that many could be very helpful in reducing pain. Perhaps some of these (and others that you may find in your research that are not listed) would resonate and be particularly beneficial for you. I will only give an extended description of these therapies but I won't discuss these in detail as that would be an entire different book.

I suggest you study these and decide if you fancy doing any. Several of these therapies can be found for free on YouTube © or other online websites.

Emotional Freedom Technique (EFT)

"An alternative treatment for physical pain and emotional distress. It's also referred to as tapping or psychological acupressure. People who use this technique believe tapping the body can create a balance in your energy system and treat pain. According to its developer, Gary Craig, a disruption in energy is the cause of all negative emotions and pain. It's believed that restoring this energy balance can relieve symptoms a negative experience or emotion may have caused." This is totally free as you can find many free videos online. Source: Healthline

Acupuncture

"The insertion of very thin needles through your skin at strategic points on your body. A key component of traditional Chinese medicine, acupuncture is most used to treat pain. Increasingly, it is being used for overall wellness, including stress management." Source: The Mayo Clinic

Acupressure

"A type of massage therapy in which manual pressure is applied to specific points on the body. It is a practice of traditional Chinese medicine (TCM) that is similar to acupuncture, except that it uses fingertip pressure instead of needles. Acupressure is said to help with a range of conditions, from motion sickness to headache to muscle pain. TCM practitioners say acupressure benefits are achieved by using pressure points along the energy pathways in the body, to encourage the free flow of energy, or qi."
Source: Very Well Health

Biofeedback therapy

This is a type of mind-body technique that is used to monitor (through connection to electrical pads) and control bodily functions, such as breathing patterns, muscle responses and heart rate.
"Without you even thinking about it, your body is constantly working on things like breathing and pumping blood. When you experience

something stressful, like chronic pain, these unconscious processes go into overdrive.
Using electrical sensors attached to your body, a biofeedback provider can measure different functions depending on your pain and its potential source. That information can help reduce your chronic pain in several different ways. It has been shown to help those with complex regional pain syndrome, temporomandibular joint pain (TMJ), headaches, ***fibromyalgia****, osteoarthritis, phantom limb pain, cancer, lupus, knee pain, whiplash, and vulvar pain."* Source: Every Day Health

Hypnosis

Hypnosis is the use of focused attention, suggestion, imagery, and relaxation to help manage pain.
"Hypnosis may be a helpful nondrug therapy to reduce pain in chronic conditions like arthritis and ***fibromyalgia****, Studies show that more than 75% of people with arthritis and related diseases experience significant pain relief using hypnosis. Far from the parlor trick of years past, today's practitioners are using hypnosis to give patients an additional tool to help manage their pain."* Source: The Arthritis Foundation

Nanotech pain patches

"Nanotechnology is a relatively new field of science. It is the study and use of incredibly small bits of matter known as atoms and molecules. Though its presence has been around for centuries, technology has now become advanced enough to be able to study and utilize these microscopic particles. Nanotech pain patches use millions of nanocapacitors to capture pain signals. A nanocapacitor is a tiny electrochemical device that stores electrical energy. The human nervous system is responsible for recognizing pain. Our nerves detect pain anywhere in our bodies through electrical signals. This pain message is then transmitted along the nerve, into the superhighway of the spinal cord, and into our brains. We then become aware of our pain. Source: Health News

Reflexology

"Reflexology, also known as zone therapy, is an alternative medical practice involving the application of pressure to specific points on the feet, ears, and hands. This is done using thumb, finger, and hand massage techniques without the use of oil or lotion. It is based on a pseudoscientific system of zones and reflex areas that purportedly reflect an image of the body on the feet and hands, with the premise that such work on the feet and hands causes a physical change to the supposedly related areas of the body." Source: Wikipedia.org

Reflexology can help reduce both acute and chronic pain from sciatica to migraines and can also help for fibromyalgia. It can also help in changing people's perception of pain resulting in reducing stress.

Reiki

"Reiki is a Japanese healing art known for promoting rest, relaxation, and the body's natural ability to heal. The practitioner simply places their hands on the body (or slightly off the body) with heart-centered intention. As a holistic therapy, Reiki works on the whole person: mind, body, emotion, and spirit. Source: Holistic Wellness Practice

TENS

TENS stands for Transcutaneous Electrical Nerve Stimulation. It is the use of low-voltage electrical impulses to relieve pain. A battery-powered device is required to deliver brief electrical bursts through electrode pads placed on the skin near pain trigger points.
"TENS can be used to relieve chronic (long-term) and acute (short-term) pain and muscles cramps from various conditions, including arthritis, ***fibromyalgia****, knee pain, back pain, neck pain, diabetic neuropathy and pelvic pain. Researchers are still determining how effective TENS units are for reducing pain. A 2013 study found that TENS was effective in relieving pain for patients with* ***fibromyalgia****."*
Source: Very Well Health

There are many other therapies you could try: Rolfing, Cognitive Behavioral Therapy, Feldenkrais Method, Guided Imagery, Intramuscular stimulation, Jacuzzi, Magnetic Therapy, Osteopathy, Chiropractor, Transcranial Magnetic Stimulation, Transdermal Magnesium, etc.

"Wake up – Kick Ass – Repeat"

Chapter 14: Step Out of Character

Stepping out of character is a great way to change what has become normal in your day and adjust the way your mind works, which will help to reduce your fibromyalgia pain.

Surprise yourself and rise above your usual character. Do something completely outside of what everyone around you, including yourself, might consider to be *"your character"* or *"your nature"*.

"Do one thing that scares you every day."
~ Eleanor Roosevelt ~

Go and do something you've always wanted to do, yet always found an excuse for not doing. While many of these *"out of character"* things may cost money, others may not, and if you have the resources, why not?

Perhaps you've always wanted to take up painting or thought you'd like to learn how to write poetry – so what if you suck at it? Go and do it anyway, because it's not about being the next Michelangelo or the next William Shakespeare – it's all about challenging yourself to do something different, no matter what the outcome.

When you step outside of your usual character, you give yourself the gift of the opportunity to experience life in a different space, at a different vibration, that may or may not be comfortable, with new eyes and childlike wonder. Giving yourself permission to do something that might not otherwise normally be within your nature helps you to switch focus and at least for a minute, an hour or a day, say, *"F*ck You"* to fibro aches and pains.

For most of us, stepping out of character is a pretty simple thing to accomplish, because let's face it, we humans are often very predictable, plodding creatures that tend to do the same things over, and over, and over again. Here's a thought – why not go skydiving – or learn how to make sushi? It doesn't really matter what it is that helps you to step outside of your usual character, just that it's a spark of something totally different for you.

When you are battling with chronic pain, taking up a new hobby or learning something totally outside of your normal day will help to break the pattern of pain you have to suffer through every day.

What's the worst that could happen when you decide to step outside of the box you've created for yourself in this lifetime? Perhaps doing something as daring as jumping out of a plane is too far outside of your comfort zone, or perhaps learning to make sushi is not as interesting as you may have thought. It doesn't matter.

The point I'm making here is to decide to do something you've never done before, whatever that may be. The only limits are what you may place upon yourself. Of course, I'm not advocating that you suddenly adopt a reckless lifestyle that places you in mortal danger just so that you forget for a moment all about the ruthless, rabid pains that fibromyalgia can bring your way.

What I am saying is that venturing down an unfamiliar path can bring you a surprising amount of relief while helping you to see just how important and special each moment in life can be. You're still here because there's something you haven't done yet. Put on your brave and determined hat and go and find out what that is.

Be courageous – never let anyone define you, and you will add excitement, vibrant color and unforgettable experiences to your life that you had no idea you really needed.

And now, to get you in the mood for a new adventure, a few words from a well-loved children's book author, Dr. Seuss:

"You're off to great places! Today is your day! Your mountain is waiting so, get on your way!"

The next page contains blank space for you to write down all the many things you may have wanted to do over your lifetime, haven't done yet or previously stopped yourself from doing, for whatever reason.

"Wake Up - Kick Ass – Repeat!"

Chapter 15: Just Say NO!

When you have decided that having chronic fibromyalgia pain in your life is not something you wish to continue with, you need to strongly fight back and believe that this is not something you are willing to put up with.

Fibro My Jackass! It's time to fight back and just say NO!

"NO, I don't accept that this life of random pain is my new existence."

Say **"NO"** when you hear that there is no cause for fibromyalgia.

Say **"NO"** when you hear that there is no cure for fibromyalgia.

Say **"NO"** when you hear that fibromyalgia can only be managed.

Say **"NO"** to only getting through the days the best way you can.

Say **"NO"** to living on pain killers.

Say **"NO"** to feeling sorry for yourself.

Say **"NO"** to giving up on all the things you love to do.

Say **"NO"** to giving up and being resigned to your fate.

Of course, nobody wants to hear from their health care provider that they have a chronic condition which they believe has no cure. However, there is a big difference between accepting bad news and actually believing what you are being told.

I heard what was said, and yet I did not for a minute believe that there was no cure and I'm very happy to say that my personal story shows that despite what the mainstream medical field might have to say about it:

"Yes, it IS possible to heal yourself! I am pain free so there IS a pain free life!"

While everyone receives and processes bad news differently, the real problem with being told that you have fibromyalgia is not the diagnosis, but rather that hearing this may affect how you deal with it.

Beyond triggering a downward spiral of negative emotions, which is what usually occurs when someone in a position of authority (i.e. a health care provider) informs you that you have an incurable health condition, is that you may simply accept this diagnosis and therefore miss out on allowing yourself the opportunity to prove this diagnosis could be entirely wrong. As with everything in your life, ***you always have a choice.*** You can accept what someone tells you, or you can empower yourself and question everything.

If after reading this book you are still finding it challenging to believe that you have it within you to treat yourself of virtually anything, including fibromyalgia, perhaps it's time to learn about what psychologists refer to as *"Cognitive Reframing"*. Let's break down what these 2 words really mean. *"Cognitive"* refers to the mental action of acquiring knowledge through thought. *"Reframing"* simply means to change the way something is experienced. In other words, when putting these 2 words together, you will be thinking about changing the way you would normally react to receiving the bad news that you have fibromyalgia.

Cognitive reframing is a technique you can learn to help you alter your usual reaction to receiving bad news. If you master the technique, you can view the situation, e.g. fibromyalgia diagnosis, and alter the way you might normally experience dealing with it. Like the power of positive thought, cognitive reframing is another technique that challenges you to identify the positive aspects of any sort of adverse event or negative news you may receive. Rather than just focusing on the negative emotions you may be feeling, you would instead look upon this news as your opportunity to try new things and explore all the many suggestions for decreasing your pain and improving your health that are outlined in this book.

When you choose to find the positive in every situation, you will be pleasantly surprised at just how much you learn about yourself, how quickly you can regain your health and how much more fulfilling your life can be. Now is the time to challenge yourself, question the fibromyalgia status quo diagnosis, take your life back, and confidently proclaim:

"I'm not interested in preserving the status quo, I want to overthrow it!"

~ Nicollo Machiavelli ~

"Wake up – Kick Ass – Repeat

Chapter 16: Weird & Wonderful Wellness

Wellness truly is both weird and wonderful because as much as we know about how to be healthy, there is just as much that we still know nothing about and that includes fibromyalgia. In today's world, there is so much marketing hype and endless contradictory opinions around health, wellness and what you should and should not do to beat the odds, that trying to wade your way through this cyclone of information, can be a stressful nightmare.

When you are actively pursuing a way to keep yourself healthy and pain free, you need to take a deep breath, be curious, have an open mind, explore, ask questions, experiment, and most of all have a sense of humor.

"You can live to be a hundred if you give up all the things that make you want to live to be a hundred."
~ Woody Allen ~

All joking aside, when pursuing wellness, it's very important to find what feels right for the amazing, unique individual that is **you.** I have personally taken many steps along my path to giving fibro the finger, and no one was more surprised than myself when I realized that the most important thing in my journey was waking up to participating in being in control of my own life. Hence, weird, wonderful wellness! I could not be happier to be now completely pain free! I haven't quite finally summarized which actions of my entire adventure should be in what order, because depending on the day, the order would often change.

For simplicities sake, I have divided the mental and physical adjustments I made in my life, the therapies I was able to avail myself of, and the potions and paraphernalia I purchased, that helped me the most and continue to, into 2 categories below: Free and Payable. I've listed them in order of the most importance to me in my recovery.

1. Free life adjustments

- A positive attitude adjustment
- Just saying NO to fibro
- MOVE more
- Slowing down in general
- Accepting change and being grateful
- Listening to healing music
- Meditation

- Cold showers
- Coloring before bed (very low cost)
- Stretching
- Reconnecting with the healing power of nature
- Laughing at myself & more in general
- Talking with a good friend
- Letting go of the guilt of not working 24/7
- Limiting keyboard time
- Taking naps
- Enjoying the little things in life
- Taking care of my fur friends

2. Payable

- EESystem treatments
- CB2 Wellness
- Foam roller
- Deep muscle massage
- Neck stretcher, balls and rollers
- Zero gravity chair
- Infrared sauna therapy
- Swimming
- Aromatherapy
- Sensory deprivation therapy
- Counselling

If you can afford it, start with trying out EESystem treatments and CB2 Wellness as I only discovered these towards the end of my fibro journey. I am convinced that my journey would have been shortened by approx. 5 months (it took me 14 months to be pain free) if I would have found these treatments earlier.

I am a writer and all through my experience with fibromyalgia I kept thinking that once I had conquered this mysterious malady, that I would write a book about my experience. I believe that thinking about writing this fibro book helped to heal me because it provided me with an organized way to take a long, hard look at my life and accept that my previous choices had created much of the pain I was feeling.

I know it may sound crazy to say that I feel grateful for having experienced such a profoundly debilitating condition. However, I really do feel that I needed this painful fibromyalgia wakeup call to give me a big push in the right direction, so that I could start being present in living my life and writing a much happier future for myself.

"Wake up – Kick Ass – Repeat"

Chapter 17: YOLO – Embrace It!

So many people get caught up in their daily distractions (such as fibromyalgia pain) and all the learned behaviors that life sends their way. They end up existing, rather than really living their life. For those of you that may not be aware of the latest, ever-growing list of acronyms that so many of us are bombarded with in today's abbreviated way of communicating, **YOLO** simply means:

"You Only Live Once"

While you no doubt have heard this expression many times over in your lifetime, for those of you who may believe that we live many different lifetimes let's just say, *"You only live once in this lifetime."*

The feeling this expression is meant to invoke is a sense of urgency so that you strive to make the very best of your life each and every day, and don't pass up opportunities, because who knows how much time you have left.

"Life should not be a journey to the grave with the intention of arriving safely in a well-preserved body, but rather to skid in broadside in a cloud of smoke, thoroughly used up, totally worn out, and loudly proclaiming, "WOW! What a ride!"
~ Hunter S. Thompson ~

I hope that you've enjoyed reading about the way I've erased fibro from my life. I also hope you've learned something you didn't know before and that you've had a few laughs along the way. Most of all, my hope for you is that you're feeling empowered to move forward with a positive outlook on how you can give Fibromyalgia the slip. You now have many ideas that can inspire you to live your very best life.

Never forget that **you have the power to heal yourself**, and that includes not just delegating fibro to the back seat of the bus but kicking it off entirely!

"F*ck Fibro – I'm outta' here."
~ Victoria B. Allen

I now hand the pen back to Christine Clayfield to write the last chapters.

Chapter 18: Are You Surprized?

by Christine Clayfield

1. How Do You Get Fibromyalgia?

You read it everywhere and the medical field also believes this: you get fibromyalgia because of past trauma, or after significant psychological stress, or after a surgery or an accident. However, I know people with fibromyalgia who never had any of these happening to them. Fibromyalgia also occurs in otherwise healthy people but most of them also have neurological, psychological or musculoskeletal problems such as nonspecific neck or back pain.

I had a lot of trauma in my past. You can read my life-story in my book: "*No Fourth River*". This book was written **before** fibromyalgia hit me like a ton of bricks. Medical professionals however told me that they don't think that my past caused my fibromyalgia as I lived "perfectly happy" for over 30 years after my traumatic times ended.

In my case, too much stress and being over-worked played a large role. There was no single triggering event for me when I couldn't cope with my pain any longer. My pain gradually accumulated over time and I ignored it and "got on with my life", resulting in, eventually, chronic pain and fatigue.

Your body is warning you and telling you to change your life and the things you are doing. Your body does this to protect you as if you don't change things, your body and mind won't be able to cope anymore and worse things are waiting for you.

Imagine your life ticks several of these points (grab a pen and tick):

- You act as if you are 20 years younger than you really are
- You are a perfectionist
- You are an A-personality type
- You are an over-thinker
- You are angry about something
- You are anxious
- You are constantly analyzing everything too much
- You are constantly tired
- You are exposed to too much Electro Magnetic Frequency
- You are generally a pessimist

- You are hunched down over phone and computer most of the day
- You are irritated quickly
- You are not in a happy relationship
- You are over-emotional
- You are over-sensitive
- You are over-stressed
- You are over-worked
- You do too many repetitive movements
- You don't drink enough water
- You don't sleep well
- You feel depressed
- You feel exhausted most of the day
- You feel nodules under your skin
- You had past trauma
- You had recent trauma
- You have a large to-do list every day.
- You have a toxic overload
- You have bad posture all day when not on phone or computer
- You have headaches
- You have immobilized muscles for long periods of time
- You have limited motion in some body parts
- You have no idea about mind-body connection
- You have pain when you move
- You have pains but just ignore them
- You have stress almost all day long
- You have too much mental stress in daily life
- You have too much noise pollution
- You haven't taken a break or holiday for 2 years or longer
- You live in light pollution
- You live in clutter around you
- You never relax
- You never slow down
- You never socialize
- You sit for too long without breaks
- You act as if life is a race instead of enjoying life to the full
- Your fascia is full of muscle knots
- Your mind never stops
- Your skin is tender to touch
- You have mood swings

Are you surprized how many you tick? Guess what! Most people tick a lot of the above points! Are you surprized your body complains and your mind is not at ease?

Fibromyalgia, according to medical professionals is thought to be related to certain abnormal levels of chemicals in your brain, resulting in your central nervous system receiving and processing pain messages wrong.

Now you've read most of this book, and probably ticked a lot of boxes, can you see that there could be a much simpler explanation? Your fascia is unhealthy all over your body combined with all the stresses and the way we live in our electronic society and that could be why your brain doesn't get correct pain messages? Something to think about!

Time to make changes in your life? I think so! I do realize that we all have to work to earn a living but please, schedule in breaks and don't work 24/7.

2. Where Do You Start?

Ok, I get it, there's a lot you could potentially do to start your recovery journey but where and how to you start?

- If you tick a lot of the boxes on the above list: change your life with the aim of un-ticking as many as possible.
- Bombard your brain with positive messages and no more negative pain messages!
- Work on a peaceful mind: do meditation or listen to calming music.
- Relax regularly
- I suggest that you do a few all-over-body stretches and see where your body feels tense. Use a foam roller on those areas and stretch again to see if it feels better.
- Schedule regular slow foam rolling sessions
- **Move** a lot more in daily life!
- Take breaks from your daily stressful life.
- Use some of the methods described in this book to get pain relief
- Believe that you can become pain free and **just say no to fibro.**

Just Say No to Fibro!

As I don't know you personally, I cannot advice you more thoroughly what to do and when to do it, but I do know that the above starting points are very important for recovery. Choose some of the remedies and treatments from this book, the ones you think you might like.

Chapter 19: What to Expect on Your Recovery Journey?

by Christine Clayfield

OK, now you've read Victoria's recovery story. What can you expect during yours? As we are all different and everyone has a bundle of different fibro symptoms, I cannot tell you exactly what to focus on physically. I do know that your attitude towards recovery will be crucially important. I hope this chapter will help you to find the right mindset for success.

Above all, remember this:

You can't control your thoughts coming into your mind but you can control what you do with those thoughts! Divert them to something positive!

If you are anxious, I found that the 333 rule worked well for me, perhaps you can try this. You can practice this any time, wherever you are: name 3 things you can hear, name 3 things you can see, and move 3 different body parts. This can divert your brain away when negative thoughts enter your mind.

1. What Mindset Do You Need Do Be Successful?

Between the life you want and the life you are living is your mindset.

a) Believe in yourself
This is **the most important mindset** you need to always carry with you, from the first day of your recovery journey.

If you want to achieve something, you need to believe in your goals and believe in yourself. Others can encourage you, but no one can give you belief in yourself. A made-up mind is a very powerful tool to have.

Don't surround yourself with people who don't believe in your goal, as they will drag you down. Don't let anybody say you can't recover from fibro. Prove them wrong.

Don't ever say something is impossible if you haven't tried it. The word "impossible" has the word "possible" in it!

b) Persistence and consistency

Persistence means to continue what you are doing regardless of hurdles and difficulties. Consistency means a consistent treatment or behavior. Consistency is what transforms being average into being excellent when you try to achieve something.

You will have to be persistent and consistent! When you are having a very painful day, you'll need to keep going and push through it. The only way you can be pain free is to use your pain as fuel for your mind and keep going. Motivation gets you going but discipline will keep you growing.

To be consistent, you need to make time to relax and realise that self-care has now become very important for you to practice so small tensions in your body do not become even bigger problems.

c) Patience

There are no shortcuts to success here! Your body is unhealthy, and your mind needs to be free of any mental stressors that might slow down your recovery. The body needs time to adjust. It's a slow process but if you keep going, you will get excellent results.

Be aware that your body will heal step by step. Don't expect to be pain free after 2 months. You might feel at some point that you are fighting a losing battle and nothing changes. Then, suddenly, things start to change, and you realise that you had 5 minutes without pain! That will be a big moment for you and it will encourage you to keep going. 5 minutes become 10, 10 become 30 and before you know it you had no pain for 2 hours soon to follow with a whole day without pain!

The most rewarding things in life are the hardest to accomplish. It might take time though so be patient.

If you are losing your patience, you are losing your battle.

d) Work hard and become a winner

It won't be luck that gets you to your end goal: free of pain. It will be hard work and determination. Anyone can get to excellence with grit, hard work and determination. Success is dependent on effort. Nothing worth having is easy to get. When you want to achieve something, strive until you achieve it. Don't accept "no" for an answer.

No one is going to knock on your front door with a pain free life presented on a silver platter. *You* need to make things happen for yourself, get the drive to overcome obstacles and become a winner. A winner will always find ways to achieve things and to make things happen.

Work hard and once you are pain free you might think, like I do now: *"Every day without pain is a good day."*

"Things always turn out best for the people who make the best of the way things turn out."
~ John Wooden ~

e) Make changes and sacrifices
Your brain's function is to protect your body from harm, wherever it can do so. Your body has warned you and made you ill by giving you pain. It is important to listen! You cannot expect to recover if you don't make changes in your life. If you don't change anything, nothing changes!

Everything has its price. You might have to sacrifice things you like, to start a better lifestyle. Have the courage to change things.

f) Be positive
Focus on the word happy or grateful every day (not just now you are reading about it) and send more happy signals to your brain. You could say: *"I am happy that I have food on the table every day"* or "*I am happy that I have a loving husband"*, or *"I am grateful for what I have*", etc.

Don't expect to say happy things for one day and then you'll feel less pain. That's not how it works. How it does work is like this: every 3 to 6 weeks your brain neurons are replaced by new ones subsequently you need to keep saying happy things for 3 to 6 weeks before you'll see changes.

Of course, I do realise that sometimes it is almost impossible to be positive and that is perfectly OK. You can be angry, sad, irritated, frustrated or anxious. These emotions make you human. We all have bad days in our lives and it is perfectly OK not to be OK.

It is the **constant negative thinking** that destroys your chances before you even start. Some people want things to happen, while others make it happen. Make sure you are in the latter group of people. **Don't**

bombard your brain with negative thoughts e.g. *"I can't do this"*, etc.

Instead, be positive and repeat these kinds of thoughts frequently in your mind:

- *"I can do this"*
- *"I am amazing"*
- *"I will get there"*
- *"I am powerful"*
- *"I am courageous"*
- *"I will be pain free"*
- *"I will keep going"*
- *"I focus on the positive"*
- *"I love my life"*

My doctor couldn't explain my pain and told me: "*It's all in your head*". In a way he was right because for a long time I focused on my pain so it **was** all in my head but not in the way he meant. 😊

So the next time you feel emotional or stressed, it's not all in your head but consider that it could be in your fascia too!

2. Don't ever give up

Whatever you are trying to achieve, remember what Sir Winston Churchill said:

"Never give up. Never give up! Never give up! Never, never, never-never-never-never!"

Make sure you never give up your fights. Rock bottom became the solid foundation on which I became pain free. It wasn't easy but I never gave up. With a strong will and even stronger belief, you can achieve great things.

Winners are not people who never fail but people who never quit
~ Edwin Louis Cole ~

Winners Never Quit and Quitters Never Win
~ Vince Lombardi ~

When life gives you a hundred reasons to break down and cry, show life that you have 101 reasons to smile and laugh. Stay strong. Never give up!

5. What is Likely to Work Best For Me?

What will work best for you is impossible to answer as I don't know your symptoms, how long you had chronic pain, what lifestyle you have, what and where you have most pain, etc.

Some people find pain relief with a foam roller, others with acceptance or laughter or positive thinking and others with changing their life completely. It is very likely to be a combination of different methods described in this book that will lead you to a pain free life.

I repeat here (for the last time 😊): **You cannot physically heal completely if your mind is troubled and not calm and happy. Negative emotions totally lock up your body if you don't process them: anger, guilt fear, worry. It all translates into body tension and that tension is stored in your fascia and giving you pain.**

6. How Long Will it Take To Be Pain Free?

Why am I putting myself through this to answer such a difficult question? 😊 I could say: *"However long it takes"* but I guess that will not give you any idea at all!

Every person, and how fibro may affect them, is unique because there are so many variables. Age, gender, current fitness, lifestyle, work environment, history of injury, emotional stress and even personality type will all influence how fibro may personally affect you.

I have absolutely no idea about you and your mindset, how often you will practice any methods, how long you've suffered from fibro pain and a lot of other influencing factors that will determine your recovery journey duration.

Over the past 5 years, I have gathered a sea of information and knowledge and have spoken to many people with fibromyalgia as well as chronic pain specialists about recovery. I conclude that, on average, full recovery is between 12 and 16 months. A lot of people feel a lot less pain (but are not pain free yet) after 6 months. A few exceptions make tremendous progress after 3 months.

Important: Don't make predictions or put a time scale on your recovery e.g. don't say: *"I will be recovered in 12 months"*. It might disappoint you tremendously if you are not pain free in those predicted 12 months. Instead, take it day by day, don't expect results too quickly.

Your body and mind are the ones that will decide when you feel "normal" again.

7. Knowledge is Power

This book (of course) doesn't cover everything there is to know about fibromyalgia recovery. If you are serious about being pain free, I suggest you self-educate yourself more: read books, listen to podcasts and watch online videos. Self-education is very important to learn more and more about causes/treatments for your chronic pain. Independent learning can produce brilliant results but also requires great commitment. Knowledge is power.

8. You Are the Lucky One!

Some people can do whatever they want and tick all the boxes under "How do you get fibromyalgia?" and will never get fibro. Others are not so lucky and get a heart attack or a stroke or are permanently depressed. You are the lucky one as you "**only**" have fibromyalgia! As far as I am aware, nobody ever died of fibromyalgia.

Don't get me wrong as I am not saying that the points under "How do you get fibromyalgia?" are the causes of heart attacks, stroke or being depressed but some points could be contributing factors.

9. A State of Mind

I love this poem by Walter D. Wintle. It expresses the timeless wisdom and power of your mindset. It is **the** most important thing to remember during your recovery: the importance of believing you can do this as success is all in the state of your mind.

It's All in the State Of Mind
If you think you are beaten, you are,
If you think that you dare not, you don't,
If you'd like to win, but you think you can't,
It's almost certain you won't.

If you think you'll lose, you've lost,
For out in the world you'll find
Success begins with a fellow's will—
It's all in the state of mind.

Full many a race is lost
ere even a step is run,
And many a coward falls
ere even his work's begun,
Think big, and your deeds will grow;
Think small, and you'll fall behind;
Think that you can, and you will—
It's all in the state of mind.

If you think you are out-classed, you are;
You've got to think high to rise;
You've got to be sure of yourself before
You ever can win a prize,
Life's battles don't always go
To the stronger or faster man;
But soon or late the man who wins
Is the man who thinks he can.

Chapter 20: Remember!

by Christine Clayfield

Well, of course, I would like you to remember everything you've read in this book but unless you have an extremely high IQ, that's not going to happen. Make sure, at the absolute minimum, to remember these 5 points though:

1. Move More!

Physical inactivity is the biggest cause for chronic pain.

2. Mind-Body Connection

Your emotional state plays a very big role in how tight your body feels. You cannot physically heal completely if your mind is troubled and not calm and happy. Negative emotions totally lock up your body. Fibromyalgia is usually a combination of mental problems and physical issue.

3. Believe You Can Achieve a Pain Free Life

This is the most important mindset you need to always carry with you, from the first day of your recovery journey: believe in yourself.

4. Don't Ever Give Up

It won't be easy and your progress might be slow but remember:
"*Winners Never Quit and Quitters Never Win*" ~ Vince Lombardi ~

5. YOLO

You Only Live Once! Enjoy the little things in life more.

I end this book with 2 pictures of frames that are in my office.

Never forget that your only limit is your mind!

Never ruin a good day by thinking about a bad day from the past. Let go!

Good luck on your recovery journey!

Christine Clayfield

Resources & References

NOTE: at the time of printing, all the websites below were working. However, as the Internet changes rapidly, some sites might no longer be live when you read this book, which of course, we have no control over.

Amazon Canada: www.Amazon.ca
UK: www.Amazon.co.uk
Amazon USA: www.Amazon.com
American Cancer Society: www.cancer.org
American Psychological Association: www.apa.org
Arthritis Foundation: www.arthritis.org
Cannanda: www.cannanda.com
Christine Clayfield: www.christineclayfield.com
Core Glow: www.coreglow.ca
DarkSky International: www.darksky.org
EESystem: www.eesystem.com
EveryDay Health: www.everydayhealth.com
Food and Drug Administration: www.fda.gov
Harvard Health: www.health.harvard.edu
Health News: www.healthnews.com
Healthline: www.healthline.com
Human Touch: www.humantouch.com
It's a Noisy Planet: www.noisyplanet.nidcd.nih.gov
John Hopkins Medicine: www.hopkinsmedicine.org
Live Science: www.livescience.com
Mayo Clinic: www.mayoclinic.org
National Association for Holistic Aromatherapy: www.naha.org
National Institute of Health: www.niams.nih.gov/health
National Library of Medicine: www.ncbi.nim.nih.gov
News Medical Life Sciences: www.news-medical.net
Peak Human: www.peak-human.com
Pixabay: www.Pixabay.com
Second Nature: www.secondnature.io
Sound Oasis: www.soundoasis.com
Trigger points: www.triggerpoints.net
Very Well Health: www.verywellhealth.com
Wikipedia: www.wikepida.org
World Health Organization: www.who.int
Yoga Journal: www.yogajournal.com

Book: *"Anatomy Trains"* by Thomas W. Myers

Published by Zoodoo Publishing 2023

Notes:

Printed in Great Britain
by Amazon

38627896R00106